SOS: SAVE OUR SCHOOLS

SOS:
Save Our Schools

Brian Simon and Clyde Chitty

LAWRENCE & WISHART
LONDON

Lawrence & Wishart Ltd
144a Old South Lambeth Road
London SW8 1XX

ISBN 0 85315 782 0

First published 1993

Photoset in North Wales by
Derek Doyle and Associates, Mold, Clwyd
Printed and bound in Great Britain by
Dotesios Ltd, Trowbridge

Contents

Abbreviations   9
Introduction   11
Letter from a Chief Education Officer   17

1   The Destruction of Local Democracy   19
    1. The White Paper and the Education Bill:
        Overall Objectives   19
    2. The Background:
        The 1988 Education Reform Act   25

2   Opting Out, or Creating a Nationalised
    System   37

3   The Educational Implications of Opting Out   52
    1. The Closing of the English Mind   52
    2. An Alternative 'Vision'   57

4   The Drive to Central Control of Education   60
    1. The Funding Agencies, Grant Maintained
        Schools and the Government's Perspective   60
    2. Other Centralising Aspects   67
        (i)   New Inspectorial Arrangements   67
        (ii) Dealing with 'Failing' Schools   70
        (iii) The National Curriculum and
              Assessment   74
        (iv) Constitutional Issues   80

5

Contents

5 The Quest for Differentiation   87
1. Recent Developments in the Politics of Choice 87
2. Furthering Diversity   99

6 The National Curriculum Eroded   107
1. Curriculum Change Since 1988   107
2. The 1992 White Paper   119
3. Special Needs   121
4. Where are we now?   123

7 Assessment and Testing: New Confrontations 126
1. Developments Since 1988   126
2. GCSE and the Future of Course Work   132
3. The Future of Inspection   133

8 The Fightback and the Alternative   137

Dedicated to the memory of
R.S. (Sam) Fisher,
1914–1992
Headteacher and life-long
protagonist
of
Comprehensive Education

Abbreviations

ACE	Advisory Centre for Education
AMG	Annual Maintenance Grant
AMA	Association of Metropolitan Authorities
AMMA	Assistant Masters and Mistresses Association
APS	Assisted Places Scheme
CASE	Campaign for the Advancement of State Education
CEA	Council for Educational Advance
CFF	Common Funding Formula
CTC	City Technology College
DES	Department of Education and Science
DFE	Department For Education
ERA	Education Reform Act (1988)
GDP	Gross Domestic Product
GMS	Grant Maintained School
HMI	Her Majesty's Inspector
LEA	Local Education Authority
LMS	Local Management of Schools
NCC	National Curriculum Council
NCPTA	National Council of Parent Teacher Associations
NFER	National Foundation of Educational Research
OFSTED	Office for Standards in Education
SAT	Standard Assessment Task
SCAA	School Curriculum and Assessment Authority
SEAC	School Examination and Assessment Council

Introduction

This short book originated in a discussion with Anne Corbett early in October 1992. We were horrified by the triumphalist rhetoric (or rhodomontade) of the White Paper, *Choice and Diversity*, published in July. Apart from its high-flown style, the paper seemed to us to fail to tackle any of the really serious challenges facing education in this country. Instead its primary purpose appeared to be to assert the primacy of a particular political party and, with that, to seek to fasten more firmly a market system on our schools. In the light of the really serious problems facing education in this country, this seemed a road to disaster.

Over the summer and early autumn of 1992, many prestigious figures, several of whom had played a key part in assisting succeeding governments (and Secretaries of State) to ground the changes brought about by the Education Reform Act (1988) within a truly educational context, issued a series of very sharp, and clearly articulated warnings as to the way things were going. These included Eric Bolton, formerly Senior Chief Inspector, and Paul Black, the original architect of the TGAT (Task Group for Assessment and Testing) report which achieved widespread acclaim from the educational world. But there were others too, for instance, Duncan Graham, first Chair and Chief Executive of the National Curriculum Council, and his

Deputy Chief Executive, Peter Watkins, both of whom had resigned for reasons now obvious. All these identified the dominant influence of the extreme right wing of the Conservative Party on policy making within the Major government as a very serious cause for concern.

In our discussion in early October the idea of publishing two books, one containing the main addresses just mentioned (and others), the other comprising our own critique of the White Paper and the (then expected) Education Bill was formulated. We hoped that others, better qualified, would undertake these tasks – but it was not to be. Time was passing. In mid-October we took the decision to undertake both ourselves. Our publishers, Lawrence and Wishart, immediately and enthusiastically undertook the publication of both volumes.

The first, finally entitled *Education Answers Back: Critical Responses to Government Policy*, containing the various addresses just mentioned, and other related matter, was prepared for the press in late October. Everyone we approached, without exception, co-operated fully in the project, making their manuscripts available at short notice. Owing to extreme pressures, two Chief Education Officers whose addresses at a seminar attended by one of the authors would have exactly fitted the book's objective, were unable to write up their speeches (both spoke from sparse notes, but also from the heart). Anne Corbett herself wrote a splendid, original chapter for this book on the English 'peculiarity' in education.

Having got this out of the way we were able, from the beginning of November, to write this book. We both feel that our schools and school systems are under a most serious threat – hence our title (used, incidentally, in an official Conservative Party pamphlet in the 1970s). The primary threat to local government, which both White Paper and Bill embody, is, we believe, a direct threat also to comprehensive schools and to comprehensive systems. As both authors have given much of their lives to assisting, encouraging, and in one case teaching in these schools, we are not prepared to see them destroyed, their ideals trampled underfoot, their support in local government swept away. Hence this book.

One of us (Brian Simon) wrote a similar critique of Kenneth Baker's Education Reform Bill (1987). Entitled *Bending the Rules, the Baker 'Reform' of Education*, it went through four editions in 1988, being published early in March of that year, just as that Bill reached the House of Lords. This book has a similar chronology, the manuscript reaching the publishers at the end of November for publication again just at the time the Bill reaches the Lords. We hope that serious amendments may be made to the Bill negating its most damaging features – this is the most that can reasonably be hoped for while we wait for better times. This book, and its sister publication, we hope, may assist that process. But even if the Education Bill passes parliament without serious amendment, the two books may, perhaps, contribute to keeping alive an alternative, and more generous concept of the role and future of education – one that will promise more hope for the future than the present shoddy enterprise.

Brian Simon drafted the first four chapters, focusing on structural issues; Clyde Chitty Chapters Five, Six, and Seven dealing with the content of education (including the National Curriculum) and with assessment, testing and the return of selection. Chapter Eight was drafted by Brian Simon after a joint discussion. Both have read each other's drafts and both take full responsibility for all that's here.

We have many debts. First, to Anne Corbett for her consistent support and encouragement for the project as a whole, and also to Martin Rogers, of Local Schools Information; whose recent book, *Opting Out, Choice and the Future of Schools* parallels our own two publications, coming from the same stable. He has been consistently generous with his unique knowledge and experience in this area. Sheila Dainton, of the Association of Teachers and Lecturers, has also generously fed us with current press cuttings and copies of relevant documents (like the Education Bill itself). Dr Robert Morris, recently of the Association of Metropolitan Authorities, and a true expert on educational legislation, has also generously given advice and help when asked, as has Ken Jones also. We owe a debt also to Stewart Ranson, of the University of Birmingham School of Education, for access to his detailed knowledge of local government affairs. On constitutional issues, which we regard as of extreme importance, we have drawn freely on the work and thinking of Ferdinand Mount and Vernon Bogdanor, and would like to thank them for their insights. We hope that they will both feel that their views are accurately represented in this volume. To Joan Simon, our warmest thanks for thinking up the title of our sister book (*Education Answers Back*) when our original proposal had to be jettisoned, and for putting up with a husband head down on helping to produce these books for a period of six weeks. To Sally Davison and Lindsay Thomas of Lawrence and Wishart, once more our warmest thanks, both for entering into the two projects so enthusiastically, and for carrying them both through so expeditiously. To Lesley Yorke, who typed both our manuscripts with great speed and unfailing accuracy, also our warmest thanks, once again.

Finally Brian Simon would like to take this opportunity to give a special word of thanks to Gordon Kirkpatrick of the University of Birmingham School of

Education. Gordon very generously gave much support and advice on the complex issues involved in Local Management of Schools for *What Future for Education?*, but owing to extreme carelessness the acknowledgement was quite incorrectly attributed in the preface of that book. This is an opportunity to make amends, and to thank Gordon Kirkpatrick for his generous assistance on that occasion, and indeed to both authors since.

Clyde Chitty
Brian Simon
Leicester
December 1992

Letter from a Chief Education Officer

We reproduce here a letter received from a Chief Education Officer. We had invited him to contribute a fine speech he made in mid October 1992 to our sister book, *Education Answers Back: Critical Responses to Government Policy* (1993). He explains here why he was unable to meet our request. This letter is reproduced with the writer's permission.

Dear Professor Simon

I am very sorry that I was unable to respond to your kind offer to give you some of my thoughts on the present situation in education. Unfortunately, because of the White Paper and the new rules for LMS, the department has been overwhelmed with work.

The talk I gave at the seminar was very much 'off the cuff' and I had no notes for that speech; even though it was ingrained on my heart. Because of the recent pressure I did not have a chance even when I returned to the office to put down those thoughts on paper. Tragically I feel that many Chief Education Officers and Chief Inspectors find themselves all too often in similar situations. If I were one of those who believe in the conspiracy theory I would suspect that the government had deliberately burdened us to keep us from critically commenting on their shortsighted and ill-advised changes. Having not responded to you leaves me feeling slightly guilty as I do feel so passionately that what is happening is not only damaging to education but fundamentally challenges the whole notion of democracy in this country. There seem to be far too few people aware of the nature of the changes that this government is bringing about. The country as a whole, and education in particular, will be the losers over the next 5-8 years.

1

The Destruction of Local Democracy

1. The White Paper and Education Bill: Overall Objectives

The vandals are after our schools. The White Paper, *Choice and Diversity* (popularly known as 'Chaos and Perversity') presages the destruction both of democratically elected, and so accountable, local education authorities *and* of our burgeoning system of comprehensive secondary schools (and a great deal more). The Education Bill, published early in November 1992, simply translates into legislative terms the proposals in the White Paper, detailing precisely how crucial powers to maintain local school systems are to be transferred to central government and its centrally appointed quangos. 'This is one of the most dramatic extensions of Whitehall power since the war', commented *The Times* in a main leader. It is a 'a devastating vote of no confidence in local democracy'. The government had decided 'to nationalise the schools . . . the powers Mr Patten is taking to himself are gargantuan' (*The Times*, 29.7.92). Nor was *The Times* the only paper to protest. The aim of the White Paper, commented a *Guardian* leader, 'is to turn all

24,000 schools into autarkic units. A national education system locally administered is to be fragmented into an amoebic society nationally administered. Chaos looms' (*Guardian*, 29.7.92). One national newspaper, however, was delighted. 'At last something to cheer about', commented the *Daily Mail* 'the revolution in education has gained irreversible momentum under John Major' (quoted in *Guardian*, 30.7.92).

Why is this government so determined to wrest power from the local education authorities? As *The Times* puts it, 'it is extraordinary that a Conservative government should have such contempt for them and such faith in the rectitude of Whitehall planning. Nationalisation will make schools more, not less, uniform' (*The Times*, 29.7.92). Many shire counties, which run school systems, are in fact controlled by the Conservatives, and in most cases these take considerable pride in their school systems and supporting services. No serious rationale has as yet been provided by this government for taking so drastic a step – one which, insidiously, appears to aim at sweeping aside a whole tier of government which, through historical and traditional usage, is and has been a crucial aspect of the constitutional set-up of the country. But of course we have no written constitution, while the present incumbent as Secretary of State for Education is well known for his belief in the supremacy and power of parliament (and has been very severely criticised for this by writers on the constitution). As things stand at present, parliament certainly does have the power to sweep away local education authorities and consign them to the dustbin of history. Whether it is wise to do so, especially with a wafer-thin majority, is another question altogether.

What is the motivation for this drastic action? The attack on local education authorities, we suggest, must

be seen as central to the changes in the school system
which this government is determined to impose. The
essential issue is clear for all to see. Since 1987,
Conservative governments, profoundly influenced by
extremist right-wing advisers, have been determined
to bring about a basic transformation of the education
system. Instead of one which attempts, however,
inadequately, to ensure equitable treatment for all,
whatever their race, class, gender or geographic
location, through the provision of common, or
comprehensive schools at both the primary and
secondary stage, the government, through creating
'diversity', is attempting to establish a structure of
schooling determined by the market. This, in the
government's view, must consist of a variety of
different types of school which, through the operation
of market forces (deployed through 'parental choice'),
will arrange themselves in a hierarchy, or pecking
order, from the 'best' to the 'worst'. For this 'vision' of
schooling to work, schools must be freed from local
authority control; they must develop as 'autarkic units'
as the *Guardian* put it – or indeed as 'little businesses'.
Hence the central thrust to achieve this ideal state
must be powerfully directed against local authorities
as such. While these still exist, the ultimate aim of this
government cannot be achieved. The more local
education authorities attempt to mollify the government by co-operating in realising specific objectives,
the more vulnerable they are to the yet heavier blows
aimed at their further destabilisation. This has been
the clear lesson of the last five years.

The line of argument here developed has been
clearly put by Will Hutton, economist, in an article on
the current move of public opinion against *laisser-faire*
policies which of course dominate this government's
thinking. Education, he writes, 'where the doctrine of
opting out and choice has been established, to make

the operation of markets in schools mimic that of the stock exchange, is set to reproduce conditions of quasi-social apartheid'. Good schools will 'overshoot' upwards and weaker schools downwards – 'just as prices do in markets' (*Guardian* 30.12.91).

This policy is very clearly designed to enhance differentiation within the school system, or, as Will Hutton succinctly puts it – 'to reproduce conditions of quasi-social apartheid'. This is the policy of the extreme right in the Conservative Party; though not overtly stated. It is, perhaps, worth noting that Eric Forth, Parliamentary Under-Secretary for Education who has the job of steering the Education Bill through the Commons, is a leading member of 'the most exclusive and dedicated band of Thatcherites' who formed the 'No Turning Back Group' of MPs ('the Malicious Tendency', Anthony Bevins, *Independent* 4.11.92). But of course extremist right-wingers have been making Conservative policy in education for many years, and still are (see Eric Bolton, Paul Black, and Judith Judd and Ngaio Crequer in Simon and Chitty, *Education Answers Back*.[1] It is important, however, to recognise that the cry for 'diversity' (or more usually 'variety') has been a long-standing Conservative Party manoeuvre to legitimise private and 'public' schools, varied forms of semi-independent church (or 'voluntary') schools and the like – including the old, discredited 'tripartite' system of the past. It was, in fact, just this type of 'variety' (e.g. the co-existence of grammar, technical and modern schools) that comprehensive education was designed to overcome. The primary aim of this move was precisely to abolish these distinctions, this crystallised form of 'diversity', which *in practice* denied fair access to educational opportunity to the vast majority of the population, in order to open up wider and more equal opportunities for children as a whole. That is why the

transition to comprehensive education was so popular
– in Thatcher's phrase, 'a roller coaster' – in the early
1970s, when Thatcher was Education Minister and
proved quite unable to prevent its forward movement.

The current attack on local authorities is being
carried through because these provide the indispen-
sable infrastructure and support for systems of
comprehensive education. To transform such systems
into something quite other (which is the objective) it is
necessary first to destablise, then to disrupt and finally
to abolish local education authorities which both
originally brought them into being and now sustain
them. The clear and precise educational objective of a
local authority has been succinctly defined by Andrew
Collier, Chief Education Officer for Cumbria. It is to
provide 'excellent educational opportunities for all' –
not for the specially chosen or selected pupils, but for
all (*Education*, 26.1.90).

It is this principle of equitable treatment that lies
behind the whole movement to comprehensive
education which, except in a very small minority of
limited geographical areas, was carried through with a
wide measure of popular support by nearly all the local
authorities in the country over the twenty year period
1960-1980. Thanks to that irresistible movement we
now have a national system of comprehensive
secondary schools in England and Wales while, north
of the border, Scotland boasts 100 per cent of
secondary schools as comprehensives.

It was not only Labour, Liberal and 'hung' councils
which turned to comprehensive education. Most shire
counties, usually controlled by Conservatives, also
voluntarily went comprehensive during these years.
Sometimes, as in Bedfordshire, this involved a split in
the Conservative Party, some of their members allying
with others to bring in comprehensive schooling.
Debates were often dramatic. But Conservative

authorities were subject to similar mass pressures as others in these years – particularly to get rid of the hated 11 plus. The introduction of comprehensive education was in fact the only practical solution to this problem. Indeed the Tory (actually, at that time, semi-feudal) shire county of Leicestershire took the lead in this whole movement, developing their well-known and highly successful two-tier system (with a break at fourteen), and being the first English county actually to abolish the 11 plus throughout its area when it opened its final comprehensive school in 1969. Anglesey in Wales had achieved this sixteen years earlier, in 1953.

The transition to comprehensive education marked a radical change of profound importance in that, as already mentioned, it established the principle of equitable funding within the whole field of secondary education for the first time in history. It is true that local variations continued in that some authorities funded their schools more generously than others as is, of course, still the case today. But within each authority equitable funding was now established. The 1944 Education Act was certainly a positive measure, but it did not achieve equitable funding in this sense (though by abolishing the separate codes of administration for elementary and secondary schools it took a large step towards it). But it was only when the divisions due to the existence of a 'variety' of schools inherited from the past was overcome with the transition to comprehensive education that fully equitable funding became a practical possibility.

The road was now clear for the development of flourishing systems of comprehensive schools now to be found all over the country. These schools in some inner-city areas have experienced difficulties, as is well known (as also did the schools that preceded them); this is a specific, and important, social problem.

But that viable systems have been brought into being, some by Labour, others by Conservative authorities cannot be denied. These are the schools, and systems, handed down to us for safe keeping and further development in the future. They represent the backbone of the English and Welsh systems of secondary education. But it is these which are now under the most serious attack.

For whatever reasons, and as stated earlier, these have never been effectively defined nor publicly presented, the government now openly states that it intends to destroy this system; to wrest from local authorities their powers of guidance, control and development, and to substitute a 'system' of 25,000 so-called 'autonomous' schools controlled directly not only by their governing bodies, but more particularly by central government itself – or whatever agents it sets up to do this job. This 'vision' (if it can be so called) involves as its central feature the destabilisation of local education authorities, leading to disruption and eventual abolition. The White Paper quite clearly states that, if the provisions of the Education Bill have their desired effect, there will be no role for LEAs of any significance once these have been deprived of their schools through opting out, so that local authorities (which of course have other functions) should dissolve their Education Committees (Cm 2021, para 6.5). Everything, it is suggested, will be run better without them. Such is the perspective. And that is the primary objective of the Education Bill (1992).

2. The Background – The 1988 Education Reform Act

Before examining the main measures in the Bill in more detail, we should recall that the attack on LEAs has been going on now for several years (more than a decade) in an attempt to construct a situation where only a final *coup-de-grace* is needed to ensure their final destruction. Much could be said about the centralising measures of the early 1980s when, alongside a ruthless policy of rate-capping directed at preventing these authorities from effectively funding their own school systems at the level *they* thought necessary, a number of steps were taken which, in effect, transferred crucial powers from the local to the central authorities. However it was only in 1987 that the growing crisis in education cried out for effective action. By this time the state to which education had been reduced, under Keith Joseph as Secretary of State, had become a national scandal. This was the outcome of years of under-funding (Joseph was a strict monetarist) and ineffective leadership which had left our school system in severe disarray. Now, belatedly, the Thatcher government and Thatcher herself finally decided to move. 'We've got to do something about education', Thatcher is reported as saying, looking to the extremist right-wing of her party for advice, as was her wont (*Times Educational Supplement*, 16.5.86).

The result was Kenneth Baker's 'Great Education Reform Bill' which became the 1988 Act. Introduced hurriedly and without any serious consultation (in spite of over *15,000* responses to the 'consultation papers' – largely critical), sharply contested in its passage through parliament, this Act laid the basis for the privatisation of the system and for creating the conditions for a market in education. The objective was to ensure the primacy of market forces in determining development and, by contrast, the down-grading and eventual supercession of LEAs and of their role in education. Here was the point – or moment – of change.

The 1988 Act, as is well known, brought in the National Curriculum with its accompaniment of mass testing (and assessment). But it also brought in new conditions affecting the running of schools as a whole. The most important of these were Open Enrolment, Local Management of Schools (LMS) and, above all, Opting Out (the new category of Grant Maintained Schools – GMS). We have argued elsewhere that these measures must be seen as a unity – a carefully designed but complete package, each measure reacting on and supporting the others.[2] The National Curriculum ensures that *all* schools (except the independent ones, which are exempt) fundamentally provide the same course of study from the age of five to sixteen (although it has already been much modified, see Chapter Six). With this in place it was practical politics to devolve immediate control of individual schools to their (re-formed) governing bodies – since no school could step out of line unless prepared to face the law. The slogan 'Power to the Parents' (more widely represented on governing bodies) was now acceptable to Conservative governments – there was little parents could do to transform the curriculum to meet their own aspirations.

Hence LMS, a reform, ironically, pioneered by as many as twenty-four local authorities (for instance, Cambridgeshire, Solihull, etc.) could be generalised and was. LMS involves local authorities syphoning a high proportion of moneys received from taxes and rates (poll tax and now council tax) directly to the schools which now become responsible for their own budgeting and so management. Parents, by this means, as members of schools governing bodies (though not a majority), appear to be being empowered at the expense of LEAs. Open enrolment, a means of creating a wider market in education (or schools) ensured that an LEA's powers to limit enrolment to particular schools to ensure that all existing schools got an equal, or at least a 'reasonable' cut of the cake, were abolished. The idea here was that so-called 'popular' schools would be encouraged to expand while 'unpopular' schools contracted and (eventually) closed. So, through the 1988 Act, market forces were deliberately substituted for the kind of planning LEAs inevitability undertook to ensure their school systems remained viable. Indeed 'planning' now became a dirty word in the government's vocabulary. So here again LEA's powers were systematically, and deliberately, reduced – cribbed, cabined and confined.

But the most crucial of these measures were those relating to opting out; indeed by far the largest section of the 1988 Act is concerned with opting out, comprising over fifty separate clauses. And this was certainly the most radical, and crucial, feature of that Act. The proposition is simple and by now very well known. Although schools have considerable direct control of their finances and management under LMS (within the given statutory conditions), opting out is presented by government spokespersons as the logical extension of LMS, involving a more total degree of independence from the LEA. Indeed, if a school 'opts out' it breaks *all* its relations with the local authority which brought it into being and in whose area it is situated.

When a school opts out the moneys which would previously have been allotted to it by the LEA are actually deducted from the grant to the authority and syphoned directly, by the Department For Education (DFE), to the school, together with an additional payment of 15 per cent of this total to compensate for the loss of LEA 'services'. This latter subtle measure both increases the income of the opted out school and diminishes the ability of the LEA to finance its services, so weakening it. A number of additional measures buttress the 'independence' of the new grant maintained school – for instance its governing body has a different composition to mainstream schools and contains no representatives whatever from the locally elected LEA. By this means the school is removed totally from the local authority's control, guidance (or assistance). It becomes, in Thatcher's memorable, if contradictory words, a 'state independent school'. This means that the school is 'independent' from the LEA, but is now *directly* subject to the state, though this is not precisely the impression that Thatcher wished to give in choosing that formulation.

We will return to the actual conditions of opted out or Grant Maintained Schools (GMS) shortly; but in the meantime the crucial point to stress is that, through opting-out, local authorities are directly weakened and rendered vulnerable specifically in areas where their significance and support for schools is most appreciated by the schools themselves. The advisory service, the provision of teachers' centres, of a school psychological service, adventure schools in the mountains, county or city wide musical and dramatic activities, from which *all* children may benefit, all these and many other LEA activities are weakened as each opted out school pockets its 15 per cent – moneys which previously went specifically to finance such central services and facilities. Through the technique of opting out, the government has very cleverly made *parents* responsible for decimating these activities – a matter which we will return to later. If *all* schools in the area of a single authority opt out, clearly that authority would cease to exist in any realistic or meaningful sense. This has not happened anywhere in the country as yet, but that this is the ultimate aim of the present government is absolutely clear. Indeed no secret whatever is *now* made as to the final objective (or solution).

This course was already presaged about five years ago by Robert Dunn, then a junior minister, in 1988, though few then took him seriously (they should have!). Subsequently other *junior* ministers (for instance, Tim Eggar, Michael Fallon) have re-iterated this objective. Now this is clearly stated as government policy in the White Paper which proposes that, at a given level of opting out, local authority education committees should dissolve themselves. This target was repeated yet again, and most publicly, in John Patten's deplorable (triumphalist) speech to the Tory Party conference in October 1992, when he said: 'I want to see all schools góing grant-maintained'. Opting out, then, is *the* weapon to be utilised to destroy LEAs (and so, their comprehensive systems). There can be no doubt of this whatever – or as Gilbert once put it more emphatically: 'Of that there is no possible doubt. No possible, probable, shadow of doubt. No possible doubt whatever.'

We will return to this issue at greater length shortly, but in the meantime we should note further measures recently taken by the government which have had the effect of down-grading local authorities and reducing their power and effectiveness in the sphere of education. In the Spring of 1991 the government suddenly announced, in the midst of a major fiscal crisis related to the forced abandonment of the egregious poll tax, that all Colleges of Further Education, including sixth form colleges, were summa-rily to be taken out of the control of the LEAs that had built them up and, for their future financing, control and development, were to be handed over to a government appointed, centralised quango. This kind of 'instant' politics, and decision-making, was in fact primarily a fiscal measure, helping the government to get off its self-created hook derived from the poll tax fiasco. A bill was rushed through parliament giving effect to this arbitrary measure (Further and Higher Education Act 1991). Local authorities, including of course several Tory controlled shire counties, suddenly found their school (and further education system) horizontally bisected, the upper half, when organised as sixth form or tertiary colleges for those aged sixteen to nineteen, entirely removed from their administration and control, being put under the aegis of the new Further Education Funding Council. Local, accountable democratic control was by this means brought to a sudden end in this important area. Acts such as these seem an unbelievable way of carrying on a crucial, and centrally important, national service.

Nor was this by any means all. That measure was not embodied in the 1988 'Reform' Act incidentally, it was a panic measure thought up later to meet a self-inflicted fiscal crisis although, of course, it chimed in nicely with the government's overall centralising policy.

It seems likely that another measure, carried through in 1992, and further weakening the already vulnerable local education authorities, was also triggered by the same fiscal crisis – the chaos caused by the poll tax crisis. Again, after no public discussion of any significance, and very suddenly implemented, the decision was taken to withdraw a high proportion of that element of central government grants supporting expenditure by LEAs on their inspection and advisory services – a total £75 million – and to allocate this instead to the centre to finance a centrally controlled, restructured inspection system. This severely threatens a service vital to the 'quality control' systems of local authorities – inspectors and advisers being the eyes and ears of LEAs with regard to the way their schools are actually functioning; it also means a very serious weakening of the LEAs advisory functions, whereby experienced and successful teachers, working as advisers, support and encourage schools in their own curriculum development and general 'process' activities. This new system, discussed in Chapter four comes into operation in September 1993. Already the great majority of LEA inspectors and advisers are under sentence of death.

This 'reform' was thought up after the 1988 Act and therefore required legislation – the Education (Schools) Act of 1992 (which also contained other measures). The 1988 Act, however, included (in one clause only) another measure weakening LEAs, though this was first announced as early as 1986, well before the 'Reform' Act was thought of. This was the City Technology College (CTC) initiative about which much has been written. This presaged the development of twenty such 'colleges' (schools actually), the capital for their establishment to be contributed largely by industry (or such was the intention) and to be situated in 'inner-city areas'.

As is by now very well known, this grandiose initiative ran into the sand; most leading industrial concerns specifically and consciously rejected co-operation, preferring to make what resources were available to normal comprehensive schools within the mainstream system (ICI is a case in point). Nevertheless the government went ahead establishing such Colleges, at very considerable cost to the taxpayer since each cost roughly £10 million to set up, only a small proportion of which was contributed by industrial or business firms. These new colleges were positioned by the government, without any consultation whatever (in most cases), within specific local authority areas, thus throwing into disarray these LEA's school supply and planning – each such College provoking emphatic and widespread protest by the authorities concerned. Baker's biggest cheer at the Tory party conference in 1986 came when he said that these Colleges would be entirely independent of local authorities. This clearly indicates their main appeal to the government – the damage and destabilisation their establishment would certainly inflict on local systems up and down the country. There is certainly a need for innovation in education and, generally, there ought to be a great deal more of it. But a statesmanlike government seriously concerned with education could find ways of encouraging such development without inflicting serious damage on the essential infrastructure of education – if it wished to.

The CTC initiative was all of a piece with the main thrust of government policy over these years. But now the 'diversity' so introduced into school provision is to be further extended as a result of new measures proposed in the White Paper and embodied in specific clauses of the monstrous Bill before parliament. New types of school, comprising new 'sectors' are now to be created – or, in some cases, are being created even before the Bill becomes law. Each of these are to be granted special funding facilities over and above those by which the great bulk of the schools are financed. These include the new 'technology schools' for whom £25 million was suddenly made available just before the 1992 election, about which there has been *no* serious public discussion or official 'consultation' whatever. These are mostly existing comprehensive schools (about 100) pulled out of the ruck and given this special status – and favoured funding. Nor is this all. A new breed ('sector'?) of schools grandiosely termed 'Technology Colleges' is apparently also to be brought into being, funded again (in spite of the CTC failure) by industry or 'business' – in this case also quite outside local authority involvement or management. The governing bodies of these Colleges are to be dominated by businessmen and women who may act as 'sponsors' – their objective, we are kindly informed, is to induct young children into the world of business skills and ethic. One such College was brought into being already before the Bill was published – at Lincoln, within a tame (and extremely backward) authority which, incidentally, is not only one of the meanest in the country (in terms of its provision for education) but also one where most of the secondary schools (for that reason) want to opt out – but that is by the way (*Times Education Supplement*, 18.9.92). We discuss these two new types of school further in Chapter Five.

All these actions – the removal of colleges of further education, tertiary and sixth form colleges from LEAs; the enforced axing of LEA inspectors and advisers; the establishment of CTCs in the heart of LEA areas – draw off the life blood of local authorities and render them increasingly vulnerable. Mass opting out is now clearly and specifically seen as the *coup-de-grace* by responsible government spokespeople. Alongside such measures, as we have just seen, goes the establishment of new types of secondary school – even new 'sectors'. So the government achieves its aim of 'diversity' – not so much within primary education as in secondary. Instead of a single type of school, the comprehensive, catering for all at least to 16 (and, incidentally, as Sir Peter Newsam recently pointed out, exceedingly 'diverse' in their character, *TES*, 18.9.92), we are to have some six or more different types of parallel secondary schools, some under local authority control and guidance (while they exist), and some not. These are (i) comprehensive schools (the great majority still), (ii) grammar schools (there are still about 150 of these, largely concentrated in Tory authorities such as Lincolnshire, Kent and Trafford), (iii) secondary modern schools (by definition in the same areas), (iv) City Technology Colleges (fifteen at present, though the original target was twenty by 1990), (v) technology schools (the terminology is now getting confused – apparently 100 already exist), (vi) technology colleges (confusion is now worse confounded, the number of these presumably depends on the degree of industrial or commercial bounty to be made available). Together with these six different types of school we now also have the big split between schools funded and controlled by LEAs on the one hand, and grant maintained schools funded and controlled by the state through the DFE on the other, laying the basis for a two-tier system. Then, of course, we have also the other big split between county schools as defined above and the categories of 'voluntary-aided' and 'voluntary controlled' schools to which, according to measures embodied in this Bill, new religious groupings, apart from the Church of England, Roman Catholics and Jews, may have access. Finally, parallel with all these, there is the private system of schooling, increasingly subsidised by the state (and so, the taxpayer) both through the 'Assisted Places Scheme' (APS) and through exemption from rates and taxes as 'charities'. This latter system, which is outside any form of democratic control or accountability, still dominates schooling as a whole as well as ensuring that mainstream schooling, while it exists, is in no sense 'national' in character.

This 'diversity', we suggest, is a recipe for chaos. It is certainly not a system designed to achieve genuine equality of opportunity and of access to the mass of the people in this country. It presages, rather, increasing differentiation and polarisation, a matter we discuss further in Chapter Five. Such, indeed, is very clearly the intention behind all the fine words, as more and more are beginning, at last, to recognise. The price of this 'diversity' is the demise of the local education authorities, and so of any form of local democracy and accountability in education.

Notes

1 *Education Answers Back*, Chitty and Simon (eds), Lawrence & Wishart, London 1993.
2 Brian Simon, *What Future For Education?*, Lawrence & Wishart, London 1992, see especially Chapters Six and Seven.

2
Opting Out, or Creating a Nationalised System

The crucial means by which this government is attempting to bring to an end the historical role or function of local education authorities, established by the 1902 Education Act, is through the measures first embodied in the 1988 Act relating to opting out. These are now being extended. The main thrust of the recent White Paper and subsequent Education Bill is to lend encouragement to this movement so that it becomes a flood, thus creating an entirely new situation. The Bill also establishes a new administrative structure for schooling in England and Wales, on the assumption of a great increase in the number of Grant Maintained Schools (GMSs). Even so, both White Paper and Bill are deeply flawed in this respect, since neither spells out with any clarity the financial implication to individual schools of taking this step. We will return to this matter shortly, but it will be as well, first, briefly to summarise developments since 1988.

The overall position at present is uncertain. In spite of strong government encouragement combined with the offer of considerable financial rewards, only 380 secondary schools (or their governing bodies) in England have in fact voted to opt out as we write

(November 1992 – of a total of 3,362 secondary schools). The proportion in Wales is much lower. A further 100 schools have voted against. In the four and a quarter years following the 1988 Act, even though an appeal was launched by post to all eligible schools throughout England and Wales almost before the ink was dry on the Queen's signature according Royal Assent, only a small proportion (11 per cent) have made a positive decision.

All middle and primary schools, however, also became eligible for grant maintained status two years ago, but their response has been relatively small. Of the 1,000 plus middle schools, a total of twenty five ballots have been favourable, ten have rejected the proposal – positive votes amounting to a proportion of about 0.25 per cent. Primary schools show a slightly more positive response, with 118 voting in favour, thirty five against, the proportion giving a favourable response reaching about half a percentage point (0.5 per cent). Totalling all these we find that, up to early November 1992, in England alone, there have been a total of 668 ballots, of which 523 gave a favourable response, 145 voting against. It is, of course, early days for primary and middle schools to get going; nevertheless the number of actual ballots held in these sectors has been low.[1]

The existing system, then, has not yet been destroyed. Far from it. The great bulk of the schools of both England and Wales remain county schools, being part of local authority systems. Over the border, in Scotland (subject to their own Education Act), *not a single school has opted out* – one tried, but ironically its application was rejected. The Scots are proud of their schools which are closely woven into local communities – and remain a powerful means for expressing Scottish nationhood. It is not unreasonable to predict that the Scots will defend their locally accountable systems at all costs.

The present government and its predecessor have unceasingly stressed the idea of 'power to the parents' in the attempt to persuade them to use their force to apply for grant maintained status – that is, objectively, against the power and influence of the LEAs. In fact, all the main parents' organisations have, *as consistently*, rejected the idea of opting out. Their main concern, as they have attempted to make clear to an unlistening government, is to build up effective systems of schooling under local democratic control – what they press for, and rightly, is enhanced and responsible parental involvement with a well-resourced local school available to parents in every area of the country. This goes for the National Confederation of Parent-Teacher Associations (NCPTA) – by far the biggest parents' organisation, comprising, as it does, several thousand parent-teacher associations, in direct contact with some 6 million parents. Parental involvement, in their view, is best enhanced by ensuring that parents' associations are established in every school. The government, though claiming to speak for parents, consistently refuses to take this step, concentrating instead on attempting to persuade parents to take the lead in opting out – a step that can be triggered by parents demanding a ballot on the issue (or by school governors doing the same). But in fact only a very small proportion of the nation's parents have shown themselves either willing or desirous of taking this step (it requires only 20 per cent of parents to do so).

The NCPTA strongly opposed opting out in the past and still shows no enthusiasm for this cause. Opting out is opposed also by the Campaign for the Advancement of State Education (CASE), an active pressure group of concerned parents and teachers, and the Advisory Centre for Education (ACE), an organisation which sets out to counsel and advise parents on school and educational matters.

Generally, then, organisations representing parents

39

oppose government policy in this area, seeking instead to strengthen parental links and influence within the existing structure of schooling. The last thing any of them want to do is to break it up, and to ally themselves with any bodies, however important, seeking this objective.

After the passage of the 1988 Act, and in spite of all the hype by the government and by government supported 'independent' bodies (the Grant Maintained School Trust, 'Choice in Education' etc.) very few schools took advantage of the new opportunities presented. Indeed the first tranche of schools to achieve GMS status were largely schools 'threatened' (if that is the right word) by re-organisation or closure by their LEA as part of a rationalisation scheme normally having the object of taking surplus school places out of action. Governments have been pressing LEAs to remove surplus places, now estimated (by the government) as 1,500,000, for years. These arise from the long-term secular decline in the child population and, of course, are expensive to maintain – the Audit Commission estimates this at £140 million a year.[2] But when authorities attempted to carry through this clearly desirable policy *after the passage of the 1988 Act* they met with a new resistance. Schools identified for closure, or for re-organisation in a new structure, could now apply for grant maintained status – that is, could 'opt out' of the authority's system, thus neatly stymying the authority's plans. And the government, supposedly charged with the care and well-being of the system as a whole, now, with Kenneth Baker still Secretary of State, coolly and calmly allowed and even encouraged schools to take this road, thus totally frustrating the legitimate and necessary plans of the authority (while also condoning the sheer wastage of public money involved in keeping the surplus school places in being).

These tactics seem almost unbelievably hypocritical. Perhaps the worst and most striking cases were those in Bedfordshire and Bath, but there were many others. Bedfordshire's plan, which involved closure of a weak comprehensive upper school, would have saved 1000 surplus places. The threatened school voted to opt out and Baker rapidly accorded it grant maintained status. In the notorious case of Beechen Cliff School at Bath, which, after a long period of consultation and public discussion was earmarked for a change in status also allowing the removal of surplus places – a plan widely approved locally – the decision to seek GMS status (which in this case was challenged in the high court) totally frustrated the entire plan. In both these cases (and many others) the natural local parental desire to oppose closure (or transformation) and to fight for the retention of 'their' school was, by this means, systematically utilised for the directly political purpose of boosting the figures of schools opting out.[3]

It is symptomatic of the state of contemporary politics that, in the White Paper and elsewhere (e.g. at the Tory Party conference in 1992) John Patten, the present holder of the honourable office of Secretary of State for Education, announces that he will personally fearlessly wield the hatchet and force local authorities to take out surplus places – as if their 'failure' to achieve this was not partly, at least, the direct result of the double-faced policy pursued by his colleagues and predecessors in that office. It seems that the Treasury is now insisting on this step. But in fact surplus places were allowed to grow to ensure success (or a 'kick start') of the opting out policy. Local authorities learnt from bitter experience not to put forward rationalisation schemes since, if they involved closure, amalgamation or change of status, any single individual school could scupper the plans by applying

41

for grant maintained status. Bedfordshire, for instance, after their experience recounted above, took a firm decision to put forward no more re-organisation plans for four years. Over England as a whole, the number of schools closed by LEAs, dropped from 612 in 1987 to only 174 in 1991.[4]

If the main motivation for the early schools involved in opting out was to avoid closure or reorganisation, other reasons operated as well. Oddly enough, Margaret Thatcher (and others) clearly believed that there would be a rush of schools opting out from what were then called 'loony left' authorities. This misjudgement simply reflected the dominance of ideology over any rational assessment of the situation. In fact, after four years, only a tiny minority of schools in these areas have opted out. The schools generally seem happy with their authorities which, in any case, no longer reflect the same political tendencies as they did four or five years ago. But what is quite striking is the fact that proportionately the largest number of schools opting out have done so from penny pinching *Tory* authorities – Kent (thirty-five), Essex (thirty-three) and Lincolnshire (twenty-three) being at the very top of the league in this respect. These are followed closely by Norfolk (sixteen) and Surrey (fifteen) both also Tory authorities.[5] The reason why it is schools in these areas which have headed the rush is clear enough. It is simply that, generally, they will be a great deal better off financially than any of their sister schools remaining with the LEA which, in the case of, for instance, Kent and Lincolnshire, are among the worst funded in the country as a whole. Hardly a proud record.

And this bring us to the main issue concerning opting out. The government has been accused of duplicity in its funding arrangements for grant maintained schools and with good reason. At the start the government assured all that there was to be a level playing field as regards funding – grant maintained schools would receive precisely the same level of funding as schools remaining with the authority, the only essential difference being that this money would come from the central authority (DES as it then was) instead of the local authority. This original policy was set out in a DES circular (21/89) as follows:

> The general principle governing the funding of grant maintained schools is that the acquisition by a school of grant maintained status should not change the financial position of either the school or of local community charge payers in the LEA which previously maintained the school. The maintenance grant from the department [for education] will be calculated so as to reflect as far as possible the level to which the school would have been funded had it continued to be funded by the LEA, including provision for services provided centrally.

When this statement was made (in 1989) it appears that the government held the view that parental longing for independence from the hated LEA would surely provide sufficient motivation to fuel the movement. But this did not occur. As we have seen, quite other motivations took precedence. And in fact the whole hoped-for swing to grant maintained status appeared after a year or two, like the CTC initiative, to be running into the sand. The government now came under increasing pressure from the extreme right wing of the Tory Party (now the policy making element) to enhance the financial inducements for opting out. Under a new Secretary of State (MacGregor), this was blatantly done. But even so things went slowly. The unexpected result of the last election (9 April 1992) was expected to result in a massive rush to opting out (John Major predicted 'an avalanche') – but this again did not occur. Now the White Paper and Education Bill introduced new measures to speed the movement; we will examine these later (Chapter Eight) – but we have yet to see how these work out.

The most decisive of financial inducements so far offered lies in capital grants (for new buildings etc.). Several years experience have now made it abundantly clear that schools becoming GMS have been treated far more generously than county schools. In 1991, for instance, GMSs got, on average, four times as much in the way of capital grants than mainstream county schools, a difference on this level has been maintained in each of the four years since 1988 (the early schools got much more).[6] Challenged on this favouritism, Prime Minister John Major, actually made a virtue of it. In a letter to Doug McAvoy, General Secretary of the National Union of Teachers who protested at this and other government measures, Major wrote:

> We have made no secret of the fact that grant maintained schools get preferential treatment in allocating grants to capital expenditure. We look favourably at GMSs in order to encourage the growth of that sector and I am delighted to see numbers are continuing to grow rapidly.

But this is not all. As well as the basic Annual Maintenance Grant (AMG) these schools receive, equivalent to what they would have received had they remained with the local authority, grant maintained schools are given several additional grants. As already mentioned they receive a sum equivalent (or reckoned to be equivalent) to the value of the central services the LEA provides for all its schools, but which GMS now have to provide for themselves (but only if they wish

44

to). This is now defined as 15 per cent of their Annual Maintenance Grant (there are exceptions; schools which opted out before 1992-3 receive 16 per cent). This sum is also clawed back from the LEA's central grant which is reduced by an equivalent amount.

In addition, GMSs receive a 'transitional grant' – a one-off payment to ease the transition. This amounts to a substantial sum; for a school of 200 or more pupils it consists of £30,000 plus £30 per pupil, to a maximum of £60,000.[8] There is also additional funding available under another category – Special Purpose Grants (SPG). These are allotted under four headings, (i) SPG 'development': annual grants equivalent to those paid to LEAs for implementing the national curriculum, staff training etc. – up to a maximum in 1992 of £42.50 per pupil; (ii) SPG 'premises': an annual grant towards the cost of insurance; (iii) SPG 'restructuring': a one-off grant schools can bid for to help with the costs of early retirement and redundancies, and (iv) SPG 'VAT': compensation for the fact that LEA schools can recover VAT on their spending but GM schools cannot. Finally, under capital grants, in addition to the main capital grant allocations already mentioned (which the Prime Minister referred to in his letter), GMSs are allocated annual grants of £10,000 a school plus £20 per pupil for small capital projects such as building alterations, improvements and equipment.[9]

From this it is possible to calculate that a 1,000 pupil school receiving *maximum* grants (excluding all SPG funds except 'development'), would receive in addition to its AMG:

Transitional grant (first year only)	£ 30,000
15 per cent of AMG[10]	£222,450
SPG (development)	£ 42,500
Capital (formula)	£ 30,000
Total:	£324,950

If, like one of the schools in the first handout (1989), they also received nearly £1,000,000 capital allocation, the total reaches over £1,300,000. No wonder one of the heads of these early opt out schools announced triumphantly 'We're quids in, we all know we are'. They certainly were.

But this was not all. In October 1990, as already indicated, pressure was put on MacGregor to speed up the process. This meant yet more money was to be made available (found, of course, from the overall budget for mainstream schools). Now the maximum level of transitional grants was suddenly doubled (to £60,000), while the levels of SPG (development) and the formula allocation of capital grants were both increased by fifty per cent.[11] This means that a 1,000 pupil school receiving maximum grant would now suddenly find itself nearly £70,000 better off during its first year than in the figures given above, their receipts arising from the transitional, SPG (development) and formula capital funding rising from £102,500 to £168,750. Overall, on the assumptions above and including one million capital (project) funding, such a school would receive a total of approximately £1,400,000 during its first year as a GMS. No wonder the comment was made in *Education* – that the road to grant maintained status is 'blatantly paved with gold' (but, at whose expense?).[12] One might add this is quite a price to pay for an ideology.

On this whole issue, the most detailed and serious study yet made, *Opting Out: Choice and the Future of Schools* by Martin Rogers, concludes that, overall, GM schools *have* been favourably treated in a number of respects, and, as the author says, 'much is made in promotional material for opting out how much better off they are, and what they have spent the extra money on'.[13] There can be no question whatever that those opting out to date are very much 'better off' – nor is it any accident that this aspect is especially stressed in promotional literature issued by government-related 'independent' organisations. Clearly generously enhanced financial support is *the* prime motivational factor in the move to opting out. It would be ridiculous to suggest otherwise. But for how long these massive hand-outs of tax-payers' money can continue to be made is another question altogether.

A recent study, financed by the *Guardian* and carried through by the Educational Management Centre of Leicester University has calculated that if 2000 secondary schools opted out, the total extra cost to the exchequer would be £300 million (if financial support continue to be given at the present rate); and that if *all* secondary schools opted out (about 4000) the total cost would rise to more than £600 million.[14] In our view this is a conservative estimate. But this is clearly why the White Paper was wary of defining what degree of financial support would be available to GMSs in the future, promising only that a consultation paper on this topic would be published in November. To date (end November) this has not appeared. The general supposition at the time of writing is that the government cannot, and is not planning, to continue supporting GM schools at the rate now obtaining – though the most recent over-excited assurances by John Patten will be referred to shortly. Of course, if there had been a rush to opt out in the summer of 1992 following the election, as John Major and others clearly expected, this would have been no longer necessary. Once in the web the schools are trapped. In actual fact, formula funded capital grants were already reduced early in the year – perhaps a portent of things to come (*Guardian*, 30.1.92).

In order to get the 'feel' of what is happening we will now look very briefly at developments over the last few months, starting with a major statement by the Prime Minister in the run-up to the election. On 18 March the *Guardian* reported that John Major put opted out schools at the top of his educational agenda (of thirty-nine steps). Major predicted 'an avalanche over a period' if the Tories were re-elected (a muddled metaphor, incidentally – the whole terrifying thing about avalanches is their unpredictability and extreme suddenness, as anyone who has experienced one will surely know). Popular schools would be given money to expand, he went on recklessly, 'regardless of surplus places in other schools' (a promise later rapidly backtracked). A month later the *Independent* predicted that there would be a sudden rush to opt out because of a growing fear that the financial plums might be withdrawn – hundreds of schools may opt out quickly, the paper reported, as many think grants will be reduced. At this point also the Grant Maintained Schools Trust announced that they were confidently expecting a great rush to opt out (*Independent*, 18.4.92).

A month later (14 May 1992), following the election, the *Independent* carried a banner headline, 'Secondary Schools will all Opt Out' before the end of the decade. John Patten was now reported as saying that many schools had held back due to the election but 'I expect now the floodgates will open'. 'It will be up to the parents to choose', he went on, at the same time threatening to stop local authorities campaigning against opting out through measures to be announced in his forthcoming White Paper and implemented in the Education Bill. 'There are a lot of authorities which are fighting tooth and nail to stop schools opting out', he said. This he would tackle head on, 'It will be one of the major parts of a White Paper we are publishing to be followed by a bill which will stop them' (*Independent*, 14.5.92).

With the issue of the White Paper two months later (in July) the argument hotted up. As we saw at the start of this chapter, both *The Times* and the *Guardian* saw its main thrust to be to increase the number of opted out schools dramatically (*Guardian*) and so to pronounce 'a devastating vote of no confidence in local democracy' (*The Times*, 29.7.92). However neither the election nor the White Paper had the longed-for effect – the latter was flawed on this precise issue as we have seen. Two months later, in September, the *TES* reported Patten's renewed attempt to stand by bribery as the main element. 'Patten will stand by cash lure', the journal reported. 'Ministers signal incentives in face of reluctance to go grant maintained'. At this point the *Financial Times* entered the fray. The schools opt out rate is low, it reported, the government's campaign has had little impact, but the White Paper appeared to signal an end to incentives (28.9.92) – this, at least, was its interpretation. In a round-up by the *Independent* at this moment (end September) the paper concluded that the negative response underlined that 'Patten's plan for schools opt out is fatally flawed' (28.9.92). Now the Tory Party was mobilised to act. In mid-October the *TES* reported a Tory drive to boost the opt out rate – 'an army of volunteers' (a 'Task Force') was being recruited. The next few months were seen as critical. Patten was about to write personally (as Secretary of State) to all schools. By this time both the Labour Party and the Liberal Democrats had, at their annual conferences, re-iterated and strengthened their opposition to opting out. Battle was joined.

Patten's letter, sent to 24,000 headteachers at the beginning of November, undated and containing a simple spelling mistake, clearly reflects a feeling of panic that the whole policy was at risk.[15] This announced that the new concern that schools becoming grant maintained would lose financially was '*totally* unfounded'; they would continue to receive 'additional funding' to 'reflect their additional responsibilities'; further the proposed Common Funding Formula (CFF) of the White Paper and Bill would not leave GM schools 'worse off than they are now' – this will be arranged so that these schools would continue to receive additional funding. After assuring heads that the proposed Funding Agency for Schools will only offer 'minimal interference' in a GM school's 'day to day affairs' the letter concludes with an assurance that certain LEA services (such as peripatetic music provision) will continue to be available to GM schools 'for a specified period of time' (the letter is disingenuous here – deliberately so? The Bill lays down a limit of two years). What effect this unusual letter has may appear over time. It is big on generalities but entirely lacking in detail or precision.

Early in November the Education Bill was given its second reading in the Commons – the debate was undistinguished and overshadowed in media reports by the latest scandal affecting government ministers (relating to covert arms deals with Iraq). It is greatly to be hoped that the Bill will pass less easily through its Commons committee stage while in the Lords it is certain to meet a robust opposition.

Notes

1 *Hansard*, 6 November 1992, pp478-88.
2 *TES*, 23 October 1992. Local authorities claim this is a substantial over-estimate.
3 For a fuller discussion of these and other cases, see Brian Simon, *What Future for Education?*, pp65-67.
4 *Guardian*, 20 July 1991.
5 *Hansard*, 6 November 1992, p514.
6 Martin Rogers, *Opting Out: Choice and the Future of Schools*, Lawrence and Wishart, London 1992, pp111-14.
7 Quoted in *ibid.*, p113.
8 *Ibid*, p103.
9 *TES*, 9 October 1992.
10 According to CIPFA annual estimates for 1991-2 (the latest available), the average cost of a secondary school pupil in England and Wales is £1,483. For a school of 1,000 pupils this amounts to £1,483,000. 15 per cent of this is £222,450.
11 Rogers, *op.cit.*, pp111-12.

12 *Education*, 29 March 1991.
13 Rogers, *op.cit.*, p113.
14 Tony Bush and Marianne Coleman, *The Financial Implications of Mass Opting Out*, University of Leicester, 1992.
15 A recent survey showed that 'sincerely' was one of the twelve words most adults cannot spell correctly – Patten, it appears, is among them. *TES*, 13 November 1992.

3
Educational Implications of Opting Out

1. The Closing of the English Mind

We should now consider some of the educational implications of the opting out policy pursued with such energy by the government. Here certain points need to be made clear from the start.

First, the whole policy is sold to the public, and grounded on the assumption, that to 'free' schools from the local authority and so establish their 'autonomy' is bound to have the overall positive effect of raising educational standards in these schools, and not only in these schools but in all others, through the edge of competition that their establishment will bring into the school system.

This assumption is itself grounded on ideology – that of the overall beneficent effect of the market. The GM school, it is held, offers a product which will attract parents as consumers of education (through their children). These parents are free to choose the best, most rewarding product (or schools). The exercise of parental choice in favour of GM schools will result in their expansion and enhancement as 'successful' schools. Obversely, market conditions will expose the weaknesses of 'failing' schools which will wither on the vine and, unless rescued, eventually close. So, it is held, overall standards are, indeed, somehow bound to rise.

We have suggested that that this assumption is an ideological construct. This is so because, to date, no evidence has been produced indicating its grounding in reality. This is not to say that no evidence is available as to standards in GM schools. In fact Her Majesty's inspectors, prior to their decimation, have undertaken an inspectorial exercise, and what have clearly been quite intensive inspections have in fact taken place in the last two years. But, unusually, no report of these inspections has been published (apart from a minor general comment a few months ago) – a matter which has excited a good deal of criticism. While it is of course perfectly possible that standards may have improved in some GM schools (researchers will be familiar with the 'Hawthorne' effect which would predict just such a development), it is hard to believe that some, at least, of the material gained from these inspections and judgements may not be altogether favourable to GM schools. It was noticeable recently that, when challenged specifically on this issue, Lady Blatch (Schools Minister) was able only to claim that GM schools were proving 'popular' (by which she meant 'over-subscribed') (*Education*, 9.10.92). That this may be so is understandable, given consistent government hype, Tory political support locally, plus their clear financial advantages over all other county (or 'maintained') schools. But there is no necessary connection between popularity in Blatch's sense, and school effectiveness in terms of raising standards.

The introduction of GM schools inevitably has a serious knock-on effect on all other schools in a given area. As each school opts out, as we have seen, so the resources available to local authorities for school services diminish. These systems, therefore, suffer – the LEA is destabilised; such, after all, is the intention. An LEA that sees the writing on the wall and is, in effect, dying, is likely not only to affect morale locally but so also the actual effective functioning of schools, often over a wide area. This applies particularly to primary schools which rely greatly on LEA support. A few authorities, for instance Hillingdon (another Tory LEA), where already the majority of secondary schools have opted out, exist only in an attenuated form – the education committee there was disbanded in October 1992 though its officials and councillors are seeking a new role through fusion with the Children's Committee. In such an unstable, and indeed threatening situation, school systems, insofar as they still exist, are operating on the edge of disaster. This cannot be good for the pupils in these schools, nor for their education.

The second point relates to this. The decision whether or not to opt out rests, through the 1988 Act, on the parents of children attending specific schools – that is, those parents having children actually at the school which has decided on a ballot. These, indeed parents as a whole, are naturally specifically concerned with their own children, with *their* educational opportunities and *their* future. They are not concerned in this way with the children in the community as a whole, with *their* equitable treatment and *their* future. Parents with children at a specific individual school are directly and immediately concerned with the short-term future of that specific school, and with no other. It is in the interests of these children that this particular school should seize every opportunity to maximise its resources, whatever the effect of this on other schools in the community. Maybe such extra resources would permit employment of another teacher in a shortage subject; improve the science

54

laboratory facilities; the library facilities, or whatever. If by the relatively simple action of voting to opt out they can assure their own children of these advantages *vis-a-vis* other children they may well tend to support this move and take this road.

As Eric Bolton has recently pointed out, this means that, instead of rational forms of educational planning carried through by an elected, and so accountable, local body (the LEA), the actual decisions determining development in any area will be made 'by nothing other than the aggregation of the random, self-interested voices made by individuals in thousands of particular schools'. This is no way (according to Bolton) of running a national educational system. 'A public education system must', says Bolton, 'be subject to some degree of overall planning and organisation'.[1]

Opting out, as at present set up, specifically appeals to parents' self-interest for its motivation, as Bolton makes clear. It does not take into account, in effect, it totally ignores the repercussions on the community as a whole of such a decision. The end object – bringing into being 25,000 'autonomous' schools, each competing against all the rest for pupils and so for resources – cannot create a 'system' in any true meaning of the term; rather a nightmare of competing institutions – each against all. Up to 1988 school systems were run as cooperative endeavours, the whole linked together through the local authority, its councillors, officials and services. No cohesion of that kind is offered in the 'vision' embodied in the White Paper and the Education Bill, nor in the speeches and publications of the Education Minister and his minions.

Finally, opting out, as shown earlier, acts as a cancer at the heart of local education authorities who are now, even against the power of the government, seeking to maintain their role locally, to restructure, re-organise and modernise themselves, streamlining their services

and deliveries, in a desperate attempt to survive and
so keep in being an organisation which can provide the
objectives of equity and social justice for *all* local
children, and so for *all* the nation's children.[2] Because
all their services are, by this vindictive Bill, under
threat. There are many things which the schools, their
leaders and children, value which can only be offered
by an organisation larger than the individual school.
County school and youth orchestras and schools of
music, whose remarkable achievements are very well
known and enormously admired across Europe (the
Leicestershire Schools Orchestra is a case in point)
require county-wide support through advisers, teachers and others. The same goes for authority-wide
dramatic activities – the achievement here of some
LEAs is remarkable. But there are other activities
outside the arts which require authority-wide support
– especially in-service for teachers and the provision of
resources and other centres where teachers from many
schools can meet, exchange experience and learn from
each other. Adventure schools, owned and run by
pioneering authorities in the Welsh and Lakeland
mountains and elsewhere provide quite new experience, especially for city-bound children, but few
individual schools could maintain such facilities.

All such services, facilities, resources, are at risk,
and as far as this government is concerned, it appears,
can be lightly flushed down the drain. The wider
horizons which enlightened education offers to
children, and which have flourished especially since
the 1960s, can be dispensed with. The Education Bill is
a philistine measure, which presages the closing of the
English mind. Its 'vision' extends no further than the
boundaries of each 'autonomous' school's playground –
unless this also has been sold off.

2. An Alternative 'Vision'

Among the 800 plus responses to the government's White Paper are several which are severely critical of the direction of policy along lines similar to our own critique. Among the most striking of these is that of the Catholic Education Service which embodies the official Roman Catholic position, being the agency of the Conference of Catholic Bishops in England and Wales.[3] Catholics, of course, provide their own schools for their own congregation and adhere to a holistic view of education as being concerned with 'the whole person – body, mind and spirit'. Their position is, of course, controversial; nevertheless it provides a specific standpoint from which to assess proposed legislation. Many will agree with the penetrating, and disturbed criticism succinctly expressed in their document, notably lacking any of the rhodomontade of the White Paper itself.

The centrepiece of government policy is now clear, the statement says. This is the grant maintained school – the determination to increase their number is noted, and the expectation that this will happen. The result will be that 'the framework of the present educational service will be gradually dismantled'.

Since only 1 per cent of all schools have been granted GM status there is much about the policy 'which is unclear and relatively untested'. It is, therefore, impossible to 'evaluate the consequences' of the government's strategies. However, as a result of preferential funding and other policies, local education authorities will be weakened, with schools 'holding ballots to ask parents to confirm the inevitable rather than to make a choice'.

The document goes on to articulate the agency's main concerns about matters in the White Paper about which they have 'substantial reservations'. The first of these goes directly to the heart of the matter: 'we do not believe that competition is a panacea for failings in education. Nor do we accept market forces as a fundamental principle in the provision of educational opportunity'. The emphasis given to these two processes, they claim, is 'inimical to true education'. Planned intervention 'is needed to protect those who are vulnerable'. In place of the emphasis on competitiveness, market forces and autonomy the emphasis should be 'on the whole person growing within a community'. Political, economic and technological considerations underlie 'the whole White Paper' – but these are quite inadequate as guiding principles for a service 'which substantially influences the development of human beings'.

The Catholic Education Service then launches an outright defence of LEAs – clearly expressing its support: 'The White Paper is severely critical of LEAs', it states, 'we not accept this almost blanket criticism. Despite certain difficulties . . . the record of our work and achievements together is one of genuine and valuable partnership'. This should not be 'lightly set aside'. Education is the concern of the whole community, 'we value the part the LEA plays in the support of our schools' and 'are deeply concerned that this partnership could be severely disrupted'.

While not opposing increased independence for schools the GM option is more than this, the statement continues. 'It intensifies financial and curricular inequalities between schools and creates new inequalities'. Further, it deprives schools of any sense of having a wider responsibility ('the common good') in the drive for autonomy. Finally the growth of the GMs sector will certainly undermine the financial viability and reputation of schools remaining outside. This will lead to a tiered system.

The paper concludes with a powerful critique of this

entire initiative which is worth reproducing in full:

> We are deeply concerned about the absence in the White Paper of a sense of the good of society as a whole, as one of the purposes of an education system and one of the criteria by which education policy should be developed. The only clear vision seems to be the centrality of individual autonomy exercised through competition and controlled by the market.

This puts our own central critique of this legislation in a nutshell. Neither of the two authors, incidentally, is a member of the Catholic Church, though John Patten is. Is it too much to expect that he take to heart these criticisms made by his own church, of a measure for which he must certainly bear ultimate responsibility?

Notes

1 Eric Bolton, 'Imaginary Gardens with Real Toads', in Chitty and Simon (eds), *Education Answers Back*, op.cit.
2 Stewart Ranson, *The Role of Local Government in Education*, London 1992.
3 Catholic Education Service, 'A Response to the White Paper, Choice and Diversity: a New Framework for Schools' (Mimeo, September 1992).

4

The Drive to Central Control of Education

1. The Funding Agencies, Grant Maintained Schools and the Government's Perspective

The destruction of local education authorities of course implies its obverse – all power to the centre, that is, to the government. Instead of a national system, locally administered – as used to be the case and to a large extent still is – we are to have a national system centrally administered. As *The Times* put it, the schools are to be nationalised – and this, by a Conservative government. 'If, as the government hopes, grant maintained schools become the norm', Vernon Bogdanor, a Reader in Government at Oxford has written, 'the Secretary of State will become responsible for the administration and funding of the schools attended by the children of 40 million people in England. No other democracy known to me organises its schools in this fashion' (*TES*, 6.11.92).

It is not only experts in government who are worried. Many have expressed horror and shock at the implications of this bid for the seizure of power. The contents of the White Paper, according to the National Association of Head Teachers, 'further haemorrhages power from parents and the local level to Whitehall and the Secretary of State. The White Paper proposes to give the Secretary of State 26 more major powers on top of the many vested in him by the Education Reform Act and other legislation' (*TES*, 25.9.92). Pat Hawkes, President of the National Union of Teachers and member of the General Council of the TUC warned delegates at a recent conference 'there is massive change going on. All power will soon be in the Education Secretary's hands' (*TES*, 11.9.92). Michael Barber has coined the phrase 'Free market Stalinism' to describe this shift, the basis of which is that 'only the government can be trusted. Hence the massive extension of central government power proposed in the White Paper'. It is a supreme irony, he concludes, 'that a government which began by declaring it would "roll back the frontiers of the state" is about to create the Leviathan' (*Education*, 11.9.92). This whole tendency, or thrust by this government is well summarised by Barry Hugill of the *Observer*, a percipient analyst of the educational scene. The present government, he says, is planning 'to replace elected local authorities with unaccountable educational quangos'. In future, the minister will have the power 'to remove governors of schools that run into difficulties; to demand the closure of schools with falling rolls or to suggest that others increase their numbers; to decide whether or not a school can bring back the 11 plus. He will have powers never before held by an Education Secretary – and all in the name of extending parental choice and reducing local bureaucracy'.[1] And so we could go on. Deep concern as to the outcome of this arrogation of power to the centre is expressed by almost every one of the responses to the White Paper we have managed to collect.

Most European countries, which have inherited centralised systems, for example France, are currently seeking means to *decentralise*, regarded as essential to release creative initiative more widely. Not so the English – or rather their government. Instead new means or weapons are being forged to bind the whole system tightly to the behests of central government, its ministers, officials, bureaucrats and (worse), its hangers on. This centralised control now threatens to cover both the structure of schooling (even if lip service is paid to 'the market') and, penetrating deeply *within* both primary and secondary schools, the curriculum and assessment (or teaching and learning). 'No other country in the world', writes Professor Paul Black, of King's College, London, 'has a system which gives such comprehensive control to its government over the curriculum with such a frequent and closely controlled system of national assessment. Thus, there are no precedents for our new systems. There are ample reasons,' he adds, speaking from his own experience, 'to be fearful about the way in which these sweeping powers may be exercised'.[2] This warning, comes from someone who was deeply involved, with the government, in designing the original scheme for assessment and testing, now through political interference, largely jettisoned or transformed. It should be taken with the seriousness it deserves.

Let us examine, first, how the Education Bill enhances direct, centralised state control over the structure of the system and its functioning. The crucial factor here of course is opting out. The government's objective here is quite clear – by April 1994 1500 schools are expected to have taken this road, by 1996 4000, but 'by then most secondary schools would have opted out' according to a Department for Education (DFE) statement which continues, 'the government hopes that all schools [in England and Wales] will eventually become grant maintained'.[3] When this happens, if it does, the entire school system will have been nationalised in terms of its administration and control.

How is the government planning this transition? It proposes to establish two 'funding agencies for schools', one for England, another for Wales.[4] These, the government claims, 'will have limited specific functions, mainly to do with paying grants'.[5] We will shortly see how 'limited' their functions actually are. The main job of the state 'agencies' however, is certainly to hand out the various grants, already discussed, to GM schools – a function now undertaken by the DFE. However these have another function lying ahead, one that has excited enormous controversy and much hostility. Totally in line with the government's own implacable hostility to local authorities, the government proposes, in the Education Bill, that, 'as the number of GM schools in any LEA area grows, the Funding Agency will share with the LEA the duty to make sure that there are enough school places'.[6]

So now a crucial planning function, clearly and precisely devolved to local education authorities by the 1944 Act, is to be removed from them, or rather to be 'shared' with a centralised quango. However, if the government has its way, it may not be shared for long. This 'sharing' of responsibility will start for secondary *or* primary pupils when 10 per cent of either of them in an LEA are taught in GM schools. According to this formula, then, 'sharing' may be the rule, say, for secondary education but not for primary, or vice versa, and this will continue for a more or less lengthy period until the next stage triggers total central control. This is defined as the point when 75 per cent of pupils (secondary *or* primary) are in GM schools. At that point, as the official document puts it, 'the whole duty will transfer to the Agency'.

Let us examine this proposition in two stages – first,

the transition and second, the position when the Funding Agencies are in total control throughout the country [England and Wales]. Some originally thought it likely that the government would set up a tier of regional councils under the central agency to ease administration – the indications are, however, that there is no such intention and certainly there is nothing in the Bill as originally published on these lines. A DFE official at a recent seminar attended by one of the authors specifically rejected this suggestion – differences between a local authority and the Funding Agency on a planning (or other) issue would apparently be sorted out by a visit to the authority by a grey suited emissary from the agency.

Two main criticisms have been made of this proposal – particularly that for the transitional period. First, that the divided responsibility will cause difficulties, disagreements and indeed confrontation and second, that a remote official body probably based in London would almost by definition lack both the local expertise and knowledge to take sensible decisions about school closures, extensions, and new school buildings – all matters with which LEAs have been most closely involved since their inception.

The proposals have come in for sharp, indeed almost unanimous criticism from responsible bodies. It is not possible to quote more than a small sample of them here. Chief Education Officers in Metropolitan authorities, who will have to operate in these new conditions, for instance, have described the transitional proposals as a recipe for 'unco-ordinated chaos' (*TES*, 16.10.92). The Association of County Councils (Conservative dominated) see them as 'a recipe for controversy and costly duplication' – they called instead for the separation of funding from responsibility for planning with 'democratically accountable' local authorities retaining responsibility for the provision of schools (*Guardian*, 28.9.92). The National Association of Head Teachers warned that, with the creation of the new Funding Agencies responsible to the Secretary of State, planning and decision making 'will become almost totally remote from local control', adding that 'there is no evidence of any coherent plan for the future of the education system' (*Guardian* 28.9.92). Commenting on the fact that the situation where both an LEA and the Funding Agency share responsibility could last a long time in many places, Peter Smith, Secretary of AMMA concluded that 'the education system faces long-term instability and chaos because of the bizarre bureaucracy created by the Bill' (*TES*, 6.11.92). With no one body specifically in charge during the transition period, commented the *Guardian*, 'a recipe has been created for buck passing'. 'Ministers seem blithely unaware of the consequences of their nationalisation of the school system' (*Guardian*, 10.11.92).

But of course this measure carries with it enormous responsibilities for detailed decisions on all sorts of issues throughout the entire country. If there will be problems during the period of transition due largely to divided responsibilities, these problems will escalate enormously if and when all schools, both primary and secondary, opt out. The problems, crises, controversies, battles, now subsumed by the existing 124 local authorities with their experienced staff deeply know-ledgeable about every aspect of local conditions and circumstances, will now land on the desks of the Funding Agencies whose constitutional position will be to act as a buffer for the Secretary of State – though, given the 300 or more new powers arrogated to the centre since the 1988 Act a great many of them will certainly land directly at his or her feet in Sanctuary Buildings. This is the burden of Vernon Bogdanor's critique already referred to.

It is Bogdanor's contention that the government's attempt to create a market in schools raises profound constitutional problems 'which seem not to have been considered'. The creation of the new Funding Agencies, he argues, 'cannot . . . undermine the vital constitutional position of ministerial responsibility'. The Education Secretary, therefore, will become responsible through the House of Commons for GM schools. The Funding Agency will be responsible for their administration and financing 'under the direction of the Secretary of State' while 'the Minister will remain responsible for policy'.[7]

In theory, then, parliamentary questions on matters of policy are legitimate, but not questions of detailed administration which can be dealt with by the Funding Agency. But, Bogdanor argues, 'every attempt to draw a line dividing the two in the case of the nationalised industries has failed dismally'. What may appear as a mere matter of detail (e.g. the closure of a small rural school) 'can have enormous political repercussions'.

It follows that, if grant maintained schools become the norm, the Secretary of State becomes responsible for the administration and funding of the entire system. This will certainly lead to severe 'governmental overload' and, indeed, such a system 'is likely to prove highly unstable'. The Secretary of State 'will find himself under pressure from a huge variety of local interests' and these will 'hold him responsible for all the deficiencies of the grant maintained schools'. If, after all, the author concludes, the Secretary of State can control everything, 'he must be held responsible for everything'.

Bogdanor concludes that the Secretary of State would be forced to devolve responsibility on to regional, or, as more effective, local units of administration. Indeed direct, personal responsibility by the Education Secretary could now be hived off if these units were supervised by locally elected members. 'That would enable the minister to escape from dealing with the problem of why Grange Road School in Giggleswick was being closed, or why the school in the High Street, Chorlton-cum-Hardy had a shortage of books.' If, Bogdanor concludes wickedly, he was exceptionally creative, the minister might then suggest that 'with local elected members supervising the local offices, these offices could be re-named local education authorities'.

So, we come full circle. The cost of the agony is enormous, not to speak of the disruption and demoralisation it entails but we have not, as yet, been through this cycle; nor can we by any means be sure that it *will* have a happy ending. Once a country takes the road to centralisation of power the process seems self-accelerating – new and more strident, or threatening means are evolved for its retention. Both Germany and the USSR in the 1930s show the truth of this. Rationality may not prevail. Better to nip any such tendencies in the bud than face the Frankenstein monster for whom the current Bill provides what may seem at first sight a civilised blueprint, but which could quite easily grow totally out of control.

2. Other Centralising Aspects

(i) New Inspectorial Arrangements

Further centralising measures include the restructuring of school inspection and the proposals in the White Paper and Bill concerning the role and powers of the proposed 'hit squads', or the oddly named 'Education Associations', in relation to 'failing schools'. It will be convenient to take these in turn, if briefly, especially since the first of these emerged, somewhat messily, in the Education (Schools) Act of 1992.

This Act, in its original form as a Bill, laid down that

schools must be inspected every four years, not by HMI (who were to be drastically slimmed down) as in the past, but by private inspection teams who would be 'vetted' by HMI. These teams had to include one member with financial and management experience, and at least one with no specific knowledge or experience of education – a 'non-educationalist'. But what raised an outcry was the condition that it would be up to each individual school to choose a particular inspectorial team 'who favoured a particular approach' (as Michael Fallon, junior minister, put it, *Observer*, 15.12.91). The money to finance this new central initiative was to be clawed back from the grant to local authorities – to the tune of £75,000,000; money LEAs used to finance their own inspectorial (and advisory) services.

This proposal, by Kenneth Clarke as Education Secretary, ran into very serious trouble. Tory controlled shire counties, it was reported, were outraged. Nine of these allied with the Labour-controlled AMA to lobby energetically against the Bill which, they believed, 'would make it impossible for councils to monitor classroom work'.[8] But in addition representatives of some twenty national organisations, of parents, governors and others, protested strongly in the press, claiming that the new inspection system was embodied in a bill 'introduced with great speed and now being rushed through parliament with little opportunity for consultation or debate'; choice of inspectorial teams, they claimed, was ludicrous – further the Bill made no provision for the follow-up and so correction of faults found. The Bill should be deferred. Liz Allen, of CASE, protested that the Bill took away the LEA's right to inspect its own schools while advisory services would also be undermined as a result of the arrogation of funds to the centre. It should be thrown out, 'lock, stock and barrel'.[9]

The Bill now ran into parliamentary timetable difficulties due to the forthcoming election. To cut a long, and typically macabre story short, it was amended in the Lords due to a successful 'ambush' by the opposition parties (the Tories had all gone home). Clarke conceded defeat on one specific issue to salvage the Bill as a whole (it contained other measures) – it was now too late to reverse the Lords amendments. The outcome was that the clauses giving schools power to choose their own inspectors was dropped. The inspectorial teams would now be chosen by the Senior Chief HMI, while LEA's would retain the right to inspect their own schools (*Independent*, 6.3.92).

This Act established the new Office for Standards in Education (OFSTED) headed by Stewart Sutherland as the (part-time) Senior Chief Inspector of Schools (he took Eric Bolton's place and combined this job with that of Vice Chancellor of London University – itself in crisis!), the staff mainly consisting of the remaining 175 HMIs. This office is to arrange the inspection of every school in England and Wales once every four years, involving the reporting on an average of 6000 schools a year, the programme starting in September 1993. To carry through these inspections, independent teams are being organised with the composition given earlier. These will bid for given inspectorial jobs but OFSTED will decide which of those bidding offers 'best value for money'. OFSTED had received some 4000 applications by September 1992 and these are undergoing training and selection. Many ex-HMIs and local authority inspectors have apparently applied.

This certainly involves a systematisation of inspection, but what sort of follow up to such inspection will be available is not clear. In the past, HMIs carried through about 170 inspections a year; these reports were published and made freely available. The 6000 OFSTED annual inspection reports will be published in three copies only. The schools inspected are to make a brief summary for parents, while they can publish the full report if they wish (and can afford to). OFSTED will also have the task of monitoring the schools examination system as a whole, *and* the implementation of the national curriculum (*Guardian*, 10.9.92).

It is, of course, far too early to evaluate the effectiveness of this initiative. Clearly there is something to be said for regular inspections along the lines proposed. But the main significance of this change, in terms of the thesis of this book, lies in the fact that this more systematised approach is being erected directly at the expense of the local authorities, who have found their own resources available for inspection reduced to the extent of the cost of OFSTED (some £75 million). This is not only a matter of prestige or the simple transfer of functions. It means that local authorities are now deprived of resources required to maintain inspectorial and advisory teams whose job was increasingly to monitor and assist what is now termed 'quality control' locally. Much might be said about this, but here the main issue only will be stressed – this step is clearly yet another major blow at the viability, and effectiveness, of LEAs (and should be seen as such).

(ii) Dealing with 'Failing' Schools

One of the most controversial measures in the Education Bill is the proposal to set up 'Education Associations' to cope with, and hopefully, turn round 'failing schools'. HMI are supposed to have handed on a 'hit list' of about 200 of these to OFSTED, said to provide the first 'targets' for inspection, but Stewart Sutherland denies knowledge of this. There are several reasons for scepticism about this proposal, one being that its covert (or, rather, quite overt) objective is simply to increase the number of GMSs without going through any democratic (balloting) procedures.

The Bill lays down a complex procedure by which a school is signalled as 'at risk'. If the Chief Inspector accepts this judgement the problem is handed to the local authority (in the case of a council school). The LEA, in the words of the government's hand-out ('Education into the Next Century'), 'will consider the action plan that the school governors must draw up, and will have new powers to take over direct financial control of the school and to appoint new governors'. In general 'an LEA will be given up to one year to get the school running satisfactorily'.

Of course local authorities do have experience in turning schools round and it has been their responsibility to exercise these over the years. The authors have personal knowledge of the extraordinary success of one such enterprise at Leicester some years ago. But an experience of this kind depends on focusing support from local advisers and inspectors, colleges of education and the local university in a concentrated way as a co-operative venture over months of hard endeavour. The Bill (and White Paper) on the other hand, is short on measures to enable LEAs to operate in this way – indeed the means by which they could so operate are being withdrawn, as we have just seen. The Bill, in fact, reflects the government's narrow managerial approach to education. LEA's 'take over direct financial control' and 'appoint new governors', but they are deprived of the means of actively assisting class teachers to operate more effectively – and normally that is precisely what needs doing. Axing some members of the 'Senior Management', as the government suggests, *may*, of course, have positive knock-on effects. On the other hand it may not.

'If the LEA does not succeed', continues the DFE

hand-out, 'the government will step in and put the school under the management of an Education Association (EA)'. This body 'will run the school until it is operating satisfactorily' (it is being suggested that they will be given two years for this). An Education Association is to be a body of not fewer than five people appointed by the Secretary of State, generally held likely to consist of retired headteachers, inspectors and administrators who 'have experience in management as well as education' (DFE document). It will be able to get government grants to deal with the problems identified at the school – 'for example, there may well need to be changes in the school's senior management team'. At the end of the period of EA management, 'the school should have made the necessary improvement'. If not, it will then be closed. But if it does (and here's the rub) it will then automatically become a grant maintained school.

Reactions to this proposal have been negative, and on a whole number of counts. 'The key to a good school is a strong head', writes Barry Hugill of the *Observer* (2.8.92). A Dad's Army 'of retired heads and former managers from industry with time on their hands is not going to perform miracles. Failing schools need experienced inspectors and advisers to point out their mistakes and draw up strategies . . . The best that can be said for the Dad's Armies is they'll come cheap'.

The National Association of Head Teachers (NAHT) has asked the government to abandon these plans altogether. It was 'unrealistic' to expect outsiders to arrest a school's decline within the times suggested. 'An outside team will not be able to establish an understanding and agree on aims and methods and implement them in such a short time'. The NAHT went on to accuse Ministers of using the recovery device 'as a deliberate back-door means of creating more opted-out schools', since rescued schools would become grant maintained without a ballot of parents (*Daily Telegraph*, 28.9.92).

More ominous, however, though entirely in keeping with the general thrust of this Bill, are the powers given to Education Associations to take over not only one, but perhaps several schools from a given LEA. Why should not two or three or even more schools in a given area be defined as 'failing'? In this case, apparently, a given EA would find itself running several schools – a mini-system, arbitrarily carved out of an LEA, even if all the formal procedures legitimising such an action have been worked through. All such schools, if 'rescued', under this Bill would become grant maintained. This measure, then, again threatens the viability of LEAs, strengthening direct centralised state control in an increasingly nation-alised system. That, of course, is the government's objective.

Our conclusion from all this underlines the general tendency of several of the measures in this Bill, together with the earlier Schools Act (1992). The proposed Funding Agencies are targeted to take over total financial control, having also enormous adminis-trative powers – acting, though, as we have seen, as buffers for the Secretaries of State for England and Wales, responsible to parliament for the exercise of these powers. Systematic inspection of all the schools in the country will be carried through by another centralised quango – OFSTED – even if its head protests its 'independence'. In the case of 'failing' schools, this body will be backed up by the proposed, centrally appointed, 'Education Associations', while any schools rescued by these bodies will immediately be consigned to the grant maintained sector to be administered directly by the state and so form part of the nationalised sector. Each and every one of these measures reduces the power, effectiveness, and indeed the very viability of LEAs. As the Germans put it, referring to Hitler's takeover of all aspects of German life and culture – the school system is being *'gleichgeschaltet'*. But, as we shall see, this tendency not only affects structural aspects of the system. Parallel procedures are being established in terms of process within these structures – the curriculum and teaching generally.

(iii) The National Curriculum and Assessment

Two bodies were set up by the 1988 Education Act, *all* of whose members *including* their chairs and chief executives (the jobs were fused) were individually hand-picked by the Secretary of State (Kenneth Baker). The National Curriculum Council (NCC) had the job of defining, promoting and overseeing the national curriculum, while the Schools Examination and Assessment Council (SEAC) overlooked new forms of testing and assessment at the ages of seven, eleven, fourteen and sixteen. It also had wider responsibilities relating to school examinations as a whole.

Both these, but particularly the NCC, were bound to follow certain consultation procedures with interested bodies (particularly teachers) before producing their final Orders, having statutory power if approved by the Secretary of State and by parliament. These embody the new curricula, including Programmes of Study, Attainment Target, and Standards Assessment Tasks (SATs).

Of course, sophisticated constitutionalists understand very well that such quangos, or buffer bodies, while giving the illusion of open consultation, serve primarily the purpose of conveyor belts, whereby government policy is imposed (while at the same time maintaining an illusion of genuine consultation and so independence). Experience over the last four years indicates that the tension between these two functions of these bodies has very rapidly tilted in favour of the conveyor belt procedure. Indeed, it was precisely over this issue that matters came to a crisis, in the case of both bodies, in July 1991.

Here is the view of one very closely involved in the work of the NCC, as its executive Deputy Director, speaking in December 1991, after various clashes between the NCC and succeeding Secretaries of State:[10] 'The independence of the council (NCC) and indeed that of SEAC is in jeopardy. The councils seem to be regarded by the government not as sources of independent, authoritative advice but are used to endorse and set out in detail what the Secretary of State has already decided to do.'

Peter Watkins goes on to discuss the nature of both the Secretary of State and the Prime Minister's detailed interference in the curriculum. As an example of the former he states that the Council's advice on the crucial Key Stage Four curriculum (14-16) 'was ignored and a new framework announced without the Council even being informed let alone consulted'. of the latter, the example he gives is the Prime Minister's announcement of a drastic reduction in coursework in GCSE. In Watkins's view, the original legislation 'clearly intended the Secretary of State to accept the Council's advice and only exceptionally to modify or reject it'. In fact, he says, he (Kenneth Clarke, in fact) 'has increasingly taken his own stance on subjects, changing the Council's advice in ways which appear cavalier'. The most flagrant example here was Clarke's decision that National Curriculum history 'should end twenty years ago'. But in several further cases recently the Secretary of State announced his own decisions when statutory consultations were still going on *on those very issues*. A number of such examples are given. 'What price consultation?', asks Peter Watkins, who understandably resigned his appointment some months earlier. 'Either the Secretary of State should announce his decision and not be required to consult or he should couch his suggestions in a broader context, inviting the NCC to consult and make recommendations'. He should, then, 'normally accept the Council's proposals'.[11]

But arbitrary decisions by succeeding (and very temporary) politicians is becoming the order of the day as the country lurches to an unconsidered centralism in its educational politics – and outcomes are becoming more and more macabre. 'My own experience of the NCC', writes Professor Black, who was deputy chair and chair of its Curriculum Review Committee, 'was that comprehensive programmes for monitoring were cut back by ministers, who have retained for themselves direct control over any research or evaluation activities of that council'. This means that any evidence of serious flaws 'cannot be forthcoming'. Nevertheless, 'the Orders in Science and Mathematics have been revised within two years of their original issue. An exercise to propose similar changes in Technology is now underway and the threat of a revision for English now hangs in the air'.[12] Paul Black was also the first chair, and inspiration, of the original Task Group for Assessment and Testing (TGAT) which drew up proposals for assessment at the four ages laid down by the 1988 Act – proposals overtly accepted in their entirety by Kenneth Baker. Experiences since have been horrific, as Black outlined in his address to the British Association in August 1992 (in a section entitled 'The Demise of the TGAT Report'). This is a story, he writes, 'of death by a thousand cuts'. Initial satisfaction at the acceptance of the report by Baker 'has been slowly but surely corroded'. Most of the undertakings given in 1989 'have by now, three years and three Secretaries of State later, been abandoned'.

Black then details each of the main issues. TGAT, he claimed, in each case won the argument. 'The chilling feature is that, in the world of political pressure to which education is now subject, that was of no consequence'. Current ideas (by implication influencing ministers) 'are based on prejudice rather than evidence, and are set fair to do serious harm to children's education'.[13]

The clash between the government appointed NCC and SEAC and ministers reached a climax in July 1991 when both Duncan Graham, chair and chief executive of NCC and Philip Halsey, a much respected figure who held the same positions in SEAC, were eased out and forced to resign. Graham has recorded his own version of these events in his recent book (with David Tytler) *A Lesson For Us All* (Routledge, London 1992). This supports the analysis we are making here. The government was now clearly determined to sweep away all obstacles from its path and transform both quangos into the submissive conveyor belts of ministerial policy it required. New appointments were now made to the post of chair of both bodies – David Pascall, a former member of Thatcher's policy unit at Downing Street (and an industrialist) moved to the NCC and Lord Griffith, described as 'the right-wing economist who headed Margaret Thatcher's policy unit at No 10 until her resignation' and appointed chair of the right-wing Centre for Policy Studies in February 1991 to SEAC.[14] Paul Black's appointment as deputy chair of the NCC was also terminated. There was, in fact, a complete turnaround in one of the most bare-faced actions of partisan politics in recent history.

In a section of his address entitled 'How did it happen?' Paul Black gives his interpretation of developments. He refers to Eric Bolton's recent speech, reprinted in *Education Answers Back*, where he draws attention 'to the overwhelming influence on current government policy in education, of right-wing pressure groups notably the Centre of Policy Studies'. One of its leading figures 'replaced the dismissed chairman of SEAC'. It is now clear, he adds, 'that the changes in the membership of the National Councils for Curriculum and for Assessment [there have been further new appointments] give each of these an increasing bias towards that particular element in our governing party'. Because of this, he adds rightly, 'the teaching profession is rapidly losing any serious respect for these Councils.[15]

Eric Bolton himself, in his address, listed by name some of the members of the small group of extreme right wingers (and their organisations) to whom this government listens (e.g. John Marks, Sheila Lawlor, Martin Turner) on issues on which they have no serious knowledge. Ironically, he said in his own address, the influence of right-wing think-tanks on the government's educational thinking appears stronger under John Major than it was under Mrs Thatcher. It is not auspicious, he concludes, 'that the formal channels of advice about education to the government appear either to be being muzzled (e.g. HMI), or *packed with people likely to say whatever the government wants to hear* (the NCC and SEAC – our emphasis, CC/BS).

These are strong words indeed. Very strong, but totally justified. The last word must go to Paul Black: 'The hopes of many that the government would exercise their sole power to appoint to the Councils in an impartial way have been sharply disappointed. Those who gave dire warnings that the Education Reform Act would be an instrument of direct government control . . . have been proved correct.[17]

As an academic researcher who saw the (1988) Act as a force for good, and who has given much of his time to trying to help its development, Black concludes, 'I am deeply disappointed and fearful at the outcomes' described in his address. 'Politicians have a legitimate interest in the curriculum', said another curriculum expert, Professor Denis Lawton, at just this time. 'But when it comes to making the system work they should be guided by those who know something about it, rather than by the ill-informed, extremist views of political advisers'.[18] That is the path to which recent legislation has driven our *educational* system.

However, if the government has its way, matters are likely to get worse rather than better. The Education Bill in fact *increases* the potential for direct control by the Secretary of State rather than reduces it. The NCC and SEAC are to be dissolved and, in their place, a single body, to be known as 'the School Curriculum and Assessment Authority' is to be established (with a parallel body for Wales). This, of course, will make it easier to 'pack with people likely to say whatever the government wants to hear', as Eric Bolton put it. The Secretary of State, of course, 'shall appoint one [of its members] as chairman (*sic*), and '*may* appoint another as deputy chairman' (will he, or she, we wonder?). This 'authority' is to consist of 'not less than ten nor more than fifteen members', all 'appointed by the Secretary of State'. Its main function, we are told, is to 'keep under review all aspects of the curriculum for maintained schools in England and all aspects of school examinations and assessment' (Education Bill, clause 215); seven other subsidiary functions are also listed in this clause. Not surprisingly, the Bill lays down that, in carrying out their functions, the Authority shall (a) comply with any directions given by the Secretary of State: and (b) act in accordance with any plans approved by him. Hardly an independent body, in any sense whatever – more a transmission system.

(iv) Constitutional Issues

The formulation just given, putting the 'Authority' for Curriculum and Assessment under the total control of the Secretary of State, sharply raises the constitutional significance of this entire exercise. A full chapter was devoted to this issue in *Bending the Rules*, since there were many who then expressed the view that the massive arrogation of powers to the centre that the ERA embodied comprised a potent threat not only to democratic norms but also to long-established constitutional forms through which educational policy was both defined and implemented. Among those expressing deep concern were Sir Peter Newsam, Tim Brighouse, then Chief Education Officer for Oxfordshire, and Dr Leonard, then Bishop of London and Chair of the Board of Education of the General Synod of the Church of England. The Board, according to Leonard 'see the maintaining of strong (and responsible) local government *as an essential element in the future of democracy in this country*'. The effect of large scale adoption of grant maintained status 'will weaken the position of local government in a fundamental way'. This is a development, he informed Kenneth Baker, 'which we would not find acceptable'.[19]

There were many, in 1988, who were prepared to give the government the benefit of the doubt – who felt that, although the ERA involved a clear centralisation of powers, these would be used sparingly and with tact, as indeed government spokespersons themselves promised at that time. Others, however, took a different view, emphasising instead the determination, already apparent, to impose full centralised control 'of almost every aspect of educational activity, at all levels, throughout the country'. Further, once these powers had been allotted to the Secretary of

State, it was argued, 'what hope is there that a future holder of that office will deliberately divest himself or herself of such powers and generously hand them back?'. To hold this view 'underestimates the steely purpose behind the legislation, and is no more than a comforting piece of self-deception. That, surely, is now very clear indeed'.[20]

This was written late in 1987. Another analysis, also made five years ago, came to a rather similar conclusion. Professor Patrick McAuslan, Professor of Public Law at the London School of Economics, introducing a section on 'The Constitutional Dimension' in *Take Care, Mr Baker*, argued that the Education Reform Bill (1987) offended against the crucial constitutional principle of the separation of powers. 'A very significant transfer of powers is being made from local elected authorities to the Secretary of State', he wrote. 'There are few effective safeguards on these powers. Such advisory and other committees and bodies which are to be established are wholly the creatures of the Secretary of State, being appointed exclusively by him.' To argue, as it might be argued 'that ministerial responsibility will provide all the safeguards necessary to expose the unreasonable use of new powers by the present or any future Secretary of State is to fly in the face of reality. Modern governments are adept at using ministerial responsibility to conceal rather than to expose'.[21]

That the 1992 Education Bill deliberately sets out to make a nonsense of the concept, and reality, of the 'separation of powers' in education cannot be denied. Ministers triumphantly foresee the eventual demise of LEAs, even if they are, at present, content to allow them a (temporary) residual role. Often they speak of them with unconcealed contempt as, sadly, many are beginning to do of parliament itself. The constitutional 'vision' of members of the present government appears limited to a crude assertion of the total sovereignty of parliament – even if Lord Hailsham once referred to the dangers of an 'elective dictatorship'.

It is noteworthy that this is the view of John Patten himself. In his recent, widely reviewed book entitled *The British Constitution Now* (1992), Ferdinand Mount sharply raps Patten over the knuckles for his concept of 'balance' in the constitution. 'The balance', Patten argued in a recent lecture, 'is one between effectiveness – the capacity of government to govern – and consent-maintaining popular support for the political system.[22] This, says Mount, 'is a bizarre conception of balance' which 'might apply just as well to a populist Third World regime . . . in which the regime, operating on no fixed principle except that of survival, yields as and when it deems prudent to popular indignation or apprehension'. But life under such a regime, while perhaps more or less tolerable, 'is not the same as life in a constitutional system which is governed by stable principles and in which power is dispersed to independent, though here and there overlapping institutions'. Talk about balance, in our political tradition, normally refers to balance between different parts of the polity, for instance, 'monarchy, Church, barons and Commons; or between government, Parliament and judiciary'. By contrast, 'the coarse monolithic governmentalist conception of balance', held apparently, by Mr Patten, 'surely demonstrates an alarming impoverishment of constitutional thought'.[23]

'Alarming' is exactly the right word. 'All power to parliament' is Mr Patten's cry, according to Ferdinand Mount – 'faintly but unnervingly reminiscent of Lenin's "All power to the Soviets"'. Both slogans, Mount argues, mean in effect 'All power to the government or governing party'. What is alien to both Lenin and Mr Patten 'is the idea of the *dispersal* of power to a variety of institutions – whether parallel, independent or subordinate'.

We have been taught, through the experience of the twentieth century, Mount goes on, 'to fear the "terrible simplifiers" and to treat all claims to total powers, in whatever name it is to be exercised, with deep distrust'.[24] One important balancing power, he argues later in his book, is that of local government now, apparently, viewed with derision by our political masters. In Mount's view, what he terms 'a degree of entrenchment' of a given structure of local, or regional government might turn out to be 'an important supporting characteristic of genuine devolution'. Such bodies should be encouraged to develop qualities of 'responsibility and durability'. This could 'help to rebuild both local pride and the local fiscal base which has been so pitifully eroded by the tragi-comedy of the poll tax'. All this would lead to greater stability and this itself would encourage improved standards of economy and administration. 'After all', he concludes, 'for 200 hundred years parliament barely intervened in local government at all; there was no need to fly to the opposite extreme in the past thirty years'. Indeed, 'the volume of legislation affecting the structure, function and finance of local government has been one of the most startling and dismal spectacles of the postwar era' culminating, one might add, in the present Education Bill. 'A great deal of this frantic and mostly futile legislative activity arises from the ease with which, under our system, governmental power can express itself in large-scale, impressive sounding legislation and the difficulty of inducing our system to consider the constitutional architecture'.[25]

That is exactly the case at the moment, and in connection with this Bill and all its works. The arrogation of all powers to the centre destroys the very possibility of balance – there is now no force, having constitutional significance, to set against, or check, the power of parliament (or the governing party therein). Government spokespersons vehemently deny this, claiming 'parents' have been empowered. But how? Parental representatives admittedly sit on school governing bodies, but these are fragmented into 25,000 separate units; they have no unified voice and certainly no representative organisations to set against and check the power of parliament. Local authorities have in the past acted as such a check – and balance – as well as giving scope for the emergence of personalities with a national reputation, able to articulate the needs and aspirations of different localities or regions. But . . . no more.

An acute observer has recently chronicled the impoverishment of cultural, political and social life in Britain, claiming a perilous erosion of democracy over the last ten years. Anthony Sampson has followed up his famous *Anatomy of Britain* of thirty years ago with a new study, *The Essential Anatomy of Britain*, recently published. He finds a widened gap between rulers and ruled – a feeling of alienation from the political system which, he says, reflects 'a real crisis of democracy'. 'Thirty years ago', he writes, 'the landscape of British power was much more varied with a wider cast of characters: rough-hewn trade unionists, outspoken professors, indignant scientists and eccentric church-men were all interrupting the assumptions of Westminster and Whitehall'. Now, he goes on, 'all the spotlights are trained centre-stage, where a single party has been in power for thirteen and a half years, led by much more mechanised politicians whose experience is largely limited to politics and finance, and who are dangerously isolated from the grassroots of public opinion'.[26]

One reason for this 'crisis of democracy', he suggests, is that during the last decade 'the traditional powers that counter-balanced government were remorselessly cut down by Mrs Thatcher – including local government, the unions and the universities, which have all been demoralised and alienated by central government'. Such has been the centralisation of power that it is 'now more extreme than in any European country', and 'without effective balances and accountability to contain it'. The most urgent remedy, Sampson concludes, 'is a deliberate delegation of powers to regional and local governments'. This can release 'immense new energies', as has been shown in France, Spain and Germany.[27] But the Education Bill, now before parliament, does nothing of the kind. On the contrary, it is yet another measure effectively transferring all serious powers from the localities and regions directly to the centre. Being carried through parliament by ministers who themselves believe that the concept of 'balance' means all power to the governing party, this Bill deliberately sets out to destroy political institutions which might stand in the way of the exercise of unrestricted power by the majority party in parliament. If carried without any serious amendment, LEAs will be tipped disdainfully into the dustbin of history. There will be no scope for initiative, in terms of the structure of the school system, inner school organisation, the content of the curriculum, even extra-curricular activities, except for those imposed from on-high by some arrogant and blustering distant politician, or an even more remote bureaucrat prepared to sell his or her soul to the highest bidder.

Notes

1 Barry Hugill, 'Patten's Dads' Army Can't Save Our Schools', the *Observer*, 2 August 1992 (reproduced in Chitty and Simon (eds), *Education Answers Back*, *op.cit.*
2 Paul Black, 'The Shifting Scenery of the National Curriculum',

in Simon and Chitty, *op.cit.*

3 *Education into the Next Century*, DFE.

4 'In Wales the Secretary of State will carry out the functions of the Funding Agency until the government decides there are enough grant maintained schools to warrant the creation of the agency. The White Paper had proposed the Further Education Funding Council for Wales would supervise grant-maintained schools for an interim period' (*TES*, 6 November 1992).

5 *Education into the Next Century*, DFE.

6 *Ibid.*

7 Vernon Bogdanor, 'Heading for Square One?' *TES*, 6.11.92.

8 *Observer*, 15 December 1991.

9 *The Independent*, 29 January, 1 February 1992.

10 Peter R Watkins, 'The National Curriculum – an Agenda for the Nineties', in Chitty and Simon, *op.cit.*

11 *Ibid.*

12 Paul Black, *op.cit.*

13 *Ibid.*

14 For the 'July events', see Brian Simon, *What Future for Education?*, *op.cit.*, pp179-88.

15 Paul Black, in Chitty and Simon, (eds), *op.cit.*

16 Eric Bolton, 'Imaginary Gardens with Real Toads', in Chitty and Simon (eds), *op.cit.*

17 Paul Black, in Chitty and Simon (eds), *op.cit.*

18 Denis Lawton, 'Is There Coherence and Purpose in the National Curriculum?', in Chitty and Simon (eds), *op.cit.*

19 Quoted in Brian Simon, *Bending the Rules*, Lawrence & Wishart, 1988, p144.

20 *Ibid.*, p149.

21 Patrick McAuslan, 'The Constitution: Does the Bill Offend It?', in *Julian Haviland* (ed), *Take Care, Mr Baker*, London, 1988, p266.

22 John Patten, 'Political Culture, Conservatism and Rolling Constitutional Changes', CPC Lecture, July 1991.

23 Ferdinand Mount, *The British Constitution Now*, London 1992, pp33-35.

24 *Ibid.*, p35.

25 *Ibid.*, pp203-5.

26 Anthony Sampson, 'No wonder Britain's In A Mess', the *Observer*, 6 November 1992.

27 *Ibid.*

5

The Quest for Differentiation

1. Recent Developments in the Politics of Choice

Former Prime Minister Margaret Thatcher never made any secret of her fundamental desire to undermine and eventually destroy the comprehensive system of secondary schooling. This could be achieved both by establishing new types of school within the secondary structure and by re-introducing (or re-inforcing) the principle of selection.

By the time of the 1988 Education Act, roughly 7 per cent of secondary pupils in Britain were being educated in independent schools, with the proportion actually being somewhat higher than that in some parts of England, notably the south east. As far as the publicly-provided system of education was concerned, as we have seen, there were still around 150 grammar schools in England and Wales, concentrated in twenty-eight LEAs. But more than 90 per cent of secondary pupils were attending comprehensive schools in England; even more in Wales; and virtually 100 per cent in Scotland.[1] This was the situation in 1988 that the Thatcher government was determined to change.

In an interview with the editor of the *Daily Mail* published in May 1987, Mrs Thatcher announced: 'We are going much further with education than we ever thought of doing before. Even though we've spent all that money per pupil, and even with more teachers, there is still so much wrong; so we are going to do something determined about it . . . There is going to be a revolution in the running of the schools.'

This 'revolution' would apparently embrace: a reduction in the powers of the local education authorities, a reversal of 'this universal comprehensive thing, which started with Circular 10/65' and 'the breaking-up of the giant comprehensives'. The Prime Minister went on to reassure her critics that: 'Not all comprehensives will be done away with . . . There are some parts of the country where they give a superb education . . . but we have to do something about choice. And choice is going to be the major breakthrough in schooling.'[2]

In an interview with Stuart Maclure published in the *TES* in April 1987, Education Secretary Kenneth Baker had also been keen to emphasise the importance of differentiation and choice:

> I want a much greater degree of variety and independence in the running of schools. I do want to see a greater amount of variety and choice . . . What we have at present is 7 per cent or so in the independent sector, probably going to rise to 10 per cent; and on the other side a huge continent: 93 per cent in the state-maintained sector. I'm responsible for that huge state sector. What I think is striking in the British education system is that there is *nothing in between* . . . I would like to see many more halfway houses, a greater choice, a greater variety. I think many parents would as well.[3]

An early example of a new 'halfway house' was the City Technology College, already referred to in Chapter One. According to the original plan, the CTCs were to be *new* schools for eleven to eighteen-year-olds established in urban areas *alongside* existing secondary schools; and they were to be *completely independent* of LEA control. Mr Baker made it clear in his speech that he had secured Treasury approval for extra public money to finance these new Colleges, but that an important element of the whole idea was that private sector sponsors would be encouraged to contribute to capital and running costs. The Colleges would be expected to develop enterprise, self-reliance and responsibility in their pupils, and would enhance diversity and choice in the secondary sector.

The idea of the CTC constitutes a significant link between the preoccupations of the Conservative Modernisers, who were particularly influential in the first half of the 1980s while Keith Joseph was at the DES and David Young was chairperson of the Manpower Services Commission, and New Right philosophy which envisages a much reduced role for the local education authorities and wants to see a far greater choice of school at the secondary level. But the link is problematic. There is a powerful recognition in the CTC concept that for too long a 'good' education has been popularly associated with a traditional academic curriculum and that something has to be done to give technical education 'respectability'. And here, as Tony Edwards, Sharon Gewirtz and Geoff Whitty point out in a recent article, the promotion of CTCs both illustrates and highlights an underlying tension between the 'modernising' and 'free-market' strands in Conservative policy. It can be argued that CTCs provide in many ways a model for how schools are intended to operate in a new market-oriented system. They have been hailed as prototypes for autonomous schools 'owned' by independent trusts and managed according to 'business principles in a competitive system. Yet as the product of conspicuous state intervention to create a suitably 'modern' type of secondary school, they may also be understood as 'recognising the limitations of the market to achieve that transformation of the labour force which advocates of modernisation perceive to be necessary'.[4] At the same time, the new Colleges pose problems for the neo-conservative members of the Hillgate Group who are forced to balance their general approval of CTCs as a 'new choice' for parents in urban areas against their hostility to the concepts of 'relevance' and 'utility' in the secondary curriculum and their objections to all 'progressive' departures from the teaching of safe, traditional forms of knowledge. In Stephen Ball's words, CTCs provide one terrain for the struggle between the 'discourse of vocational progressivism' and 'the elitist conceptions of knowledge proselytised by the old humanists'.[5]

As far as the selection of pupils is concerned, there are guidelines laid down in the original glossy promotional brochure *City Technology Colleges: A New Choice of School* published by the DES in October 1986:

> Each CTC will serve a substantial catchment area. The composition of their intake will be representative of the community they serve. They will not be neighbourhood schools taking all comers; nor will they be expected to admit children from outside the catchment area. Their admission procedures and catchment areas will need to be defined in such a way as to give scope for selecting pupils from a number of applicants. The precise arrangements will need to be decided case-by-case, but a typical catchment area is

likely to contain at least 5,000 pupils of secondary age, from whom 750-1,000 pupils will be admitted.[6]

From all this, it seems clear that CTCs are statutorily obliged to show intakes 'representative of the community they serve'. Yet the limited amount of research that has been carried out into the CTC development shows that the Colleges are viewed as elitist institutions in the area which they serve and generally act as powerful agents for upward mobility among working-class children. The reason for this would seem to lie in the selection process. For as the 1986 brochure makes clear:

> Pupils will be selected by the head and governing body on the basis of their general attitude, for example as reflected in their progress and achievements at primary school; on their readiness to take advantage of the type of education offered in CTCs; and on their parents' commitment to full-time education or training up to the age of 18, to the distinctive characteristics of the CTC curriculum, and to the ethos of the CTC . . . A prime consideration in the selection of pupils will be whether they are likely to benefit from what the CTC offers.[7]

And on the basis of their research at Kingshurst in Solihull, the first of the CTCs to be opened, Geoffrey Walford and Henry Miller have argued that, whatever their commitment to being comprehensive, selection procedures which include written tests and interviews may well link the new CTCs in the minds of parents with the 'quality' previously associated with a grammar school education and convince the successful pupils that they have been chosen on merit.[8]

The second 'halfway house' (to use Kenneth Baker's terminology) is the grant maintained school; and a key proposal in the 1988 Education Act was, of course to allow (indeed encourage) schools to opt out of local authority control and become (in Mrs Thatcher's phrase) 'independent state schools'. We have already looked at this development at some length in the light of the further proposals outlined in the 1992 White Paper and the Education Bill. In this chapter we concentrate on the likely impact of the change on the future development of comprehensive schooling.

From the very beginning, there was considerable confusion as to how grant-maintained schools in the secondary sector would differ from neighbouring comprehensives. Would they be selective? Would there be a fee-paying element? Would the government allow them to modify the rigid curriculum framework laid down in the 1988 Act?

Junior education minister Bob Dunn proudly announced to a meeting of right-wing supporters of the Conservative Party in May 1987 that new government proposals to allow schools to take as many pupils as they could physically cope with, in tandem with the plans to give headteachers control of school budgets and the right, given certain safeguards, to take their schools out of local council control, were all parts of a grand strategy that would eventually lead to 'the denationalisation of education'. And at a pre-election press conference in May 1987, Margaret Thatcher argued that heads and governors who 'opted out' of local authority control should be free to establish their own admissions policies, and would not necessarily be prevented from raising extra funds through parents – thereby giving rise to much media speculation that the new plans might well include a fee-paying element.[10] Indeed, Kenneth Baker conceded during a BBC Radio *World at One* discussion broadcast on 10 June 1987 that there would be nothing to stop 'better-off parents' raising additional resources for a particular 'opted out' school, so that the headteacher would then be able to purchase particularly expensive books and items of equipment and perhaps even pay some of the teachers higher salaries. Later DES statements during the Summer, however, were anxious to play down the fee-paying aspect and even to deny that the 'opting out' proposal was really a covert means of re-introducing secondary selection.

Confusion reigned throughout the Autumn of 1987, with Kenneth Baker now making a determined effort to preserve a certain degree of independence for the DES machine. In an interview with the *Independent*, published in September 1987, Mrs Thatcher looked forward to a situation where 'most secondary schools' would choose to opt out of the locally administered state system[11] whereas Mr Baker argued on television in November that, in his opinion, only a minority of schools would choose to go down that path.[12] Mrs Thatcher hoped that popular comprehensive schools which opted out of the system would soon elect to 'change their character' and become selective; whereas Mr Baker said he expected most comprehensives would choose to remain comprehensive.[13]

As the 1987 Bill was being drafted, there was an assurance from Mr Baker that no proposal for a change of character would be entertained within five years of a school acquiring grant-maintained status. This stipulation did not actually appear in the Bill itself; but it was bitterly resented by the right-wing think-tanks. It was formally abandoned by Kenneth Clarke on 25 April 1991.

By the Spring of 1991, the Major government was anxious to make it clear that opt out schools could turn themselves into grammar schools without too much difficulty. Mr Clarke said he was not unduly worried if his critics viewed the opt out policy as 'a back-door attempt to re-introduce grammar schools'. Alternatively, he would be quite happy if grant maintained schools decided to become 'magnet schools'. Pupils would then be admitted on the basis of 'their aptitude for specific subjects such as science or technology or art and design'.[14]

The Education Secretary used the BBC's *On The Record* programme at the beginning of February 1992 to emphasise to Tory 'hardliners' that the Major government would like to see the return of grammar schools, as part of a more diverse state education system. On this occasion he indicated that he would have 'no problem with one grant-maintained school in ten becoming a new grammar school'. He made it clear that grammar schools could re-appear throughout the country as long as there were not too many in each area. The government, he said, was simply anxious to respond to local pressures:

We have no objection to the re-emergence of grammar schools, if that is what the parents want ... Parents will decide; schools will decide ... I am simply responding to their demands as they set out the separate characteristics they want to adopt ... The stigma attached to secondary modern schools will be avoided through the growth of magnet schools: technological schools and others with different specialisms ... We have got to get away from the idea that the only good education is, in fact, an academic education, and that the only good qualification is an academic one.[15]

Robert Balchin, chairperson of the Grant Maintained Schools' Trust, responded to Mr Clarke's comments by saying that he confidently expected that between five and ten per cent of schools opting out would choose to become selective. After all, there was nothing shameful in the idea of 11-plus selection: 'a school builds up a specific kind of ethos, and some children will not be suited to that particular ethos, so it is right that they should not be allowed to go there'. And Lord Griffiths of Fforestfach, chairperson of the School Examinations and Assessment Council, commented: 'if you give parents real choice in the system, it is inevitable that the schools themselves will demand to choose the kind of pupils that come'[17] – a remark which would seem to bear out the view often expressed on the left that in a market system, *schools choose parents*, not the other way round. At the same time, research carried out by a team at the University of Leicester and published in 1992 reveals that a third of the first comprehensive schools to opt out have used some form of selection when over-subscribed, without going through the process of applying for a change of character.[18]

The search for new types of schools at the secondary level is clearly indicative of the right's long-standing and profound hostility to the comprehensive principle. And Conservative politicians find it useful to ignore the remarkable degree of success that comprehensive schools have had in a number of areas.

Using examination results as a very narrow (though nonetheless important) criterion of success, the DES White Paper *Better Schools*, published in March 1985, reported that one in five students was now gaining at least one 'A'-level pass, compared with only one in seven (14 per cent) during the 1960s; and over a quarter of pupils (27 per cent) were now obtaining five 'O' level 'pass' equivalents, against only a fifth twenty or so years before.[19] And in his Presidential Address to the Education Section of the British Association for the Advancement of Science, delivered in August 1992,

Professor Paul Black pointed out that between 1970-71 and 1989-90, the percentage of pupils leaving school with no graded examination results fell from 44 per cent to 8.3 per cent (due in part, of course, to the raising of the school leaving age to sixteen in 1972-73); while the percentage gaining five or more higher grades at GCSE or the equivalents rose from 7.1 per cent to 11.4 per cent.[20]

As a result of their large-scale research into the effects of comprehensive re-organisation in Scotland, McPherson and Willms concluded at the end of the 1980s that: 'Since the mid-1970s, the reorganisation that was initiated in 1965 has contributed both to a rise in examination attainment and to a fall in the effect on attainment of social class. We call these two trends respectively: 'improvement' and 'equalisation'.'[21]

And their meticulous review of the impact of comprehensive reorganisation in Britain led Glennerster and Low to conclude in 1990 that: 'The main and really major improvements in examination performance were achieved by the average-ability students, and they were achieved mostly in the comprehensive schools . . . It is a tribute to the state schools that they produced both more qualified leavers and the structural changes politicians were demanding.'[22]

All this is conveniently ignored by the new Prime Minister who seems determined to resurrect all the harmful characteristics of the divided system of the 1950s and early 1960s. Indeed, Mr Major seems happy to disregard all the evidence that the postwar secondary structure did untold harm to the future prospects of the vast majority of the nation's children. And this attitude is iniquitous, for as Tony Mooney, Head of Rutlish School in Merton, pointed out in an article in *Education* in November 1992:

The old tripartite system of grammar, technical and secondary modern schools was one of the most efficient stiflers of educational potential ever devised. By selecting children for these schools at the age of 11, on the basis of spurious IQ tests, the system ensured that 80 per cent of the school population was directed to the low-status secondary modern schools. Those who attended these schools regarded themselves as educational failures and were caught in a trap from which it was difficult to escape.[23]

The Prime Minister sees things very differently, as he made clear in his speech to the Centre for Policy Studies delivered at the Café Royal in London in July 1991. According to Mr Major, the left's obsession with comprehensive re-organisation in the 1960s was based on a 'mania for equality'.

This was equality not of *opportunity*, but of *outcome*. This was a mania that condemned children to fall short of their potential; that treated them as if they were identical – or must be made so. A mania that undermined common sense values in schools, rejected proven teaching methods, debased standards – or disposed of them altogether. A canker in our education system which spread from the 1960s on, and deprived great cohorts of our children of the opportunities they deserved. I, for one, cannot find it easy to forgive the left for that.[24]

John Major's obsessive hostility towards comprehensive schooling was further emphasised in a four-page letter to Fred Jarvis, former general secretary of the NUT, released to the press at the end of February 1992. In this remarkably frank letter, which was more outspoken than any of the pronouncements of the then Education Secretary Kenneth Clarke, the Prime Minister seemed anxious to blame our comprehensive schools for *all* the failings of the education system, in a crude blanket condemnation which accused the Labour Party of having introduced a secondary structure which fostered low standards and expectations:

> I am drawn to the view that the problem of low standards stems in large part from the nature of the comprehensive system which the Labour Party ushered in in the 1960s, and from the intellectual climate underpinning it that has tended to stress equality of *outcome* at the expense of equality of *opportunity*.
>
> The orthodoxy which has grown up around the comprehensive system has, frankly, been an orthodoxy of the left: hostility to competition *between* schools and *between* pupils, and even in sport; hostility to testing; hostility to genuine parental choice; and a steady infiltration of traditional curriculum subjects such as history and English literature by some questionable dogmas that fly in the face of common sense.
>
> I ask you not to doubt my sincerity and determination to reverse the failings of the comprehensive system and the cycle of low expectations and low standards which it has fostered.[25]

Education Secretary John Patten has also seen fit to ridicule the 'progressive' aspirations of the left in the 1960s; and he has argued in an article published in *New Statesman and Society* in July 1992 that Labour's Tony Crosland tried to throw out 'human nature – individualism and specialisation in particular – with the anti-selection bath water'.

Crosland ... thought that there should be equality of opportunity. He was, however, wrong about what are so tiresomely called the educational delivery mechanisms. You do *not* liberate talents and open doors for young people by treating everyone the same. Children have different skills, talents, abilities, interests and ambitions ... It seems to me that the left's refusal to recognise that diversity and individuality exist has led to Labour's educational aeroplanes nose-diving every time.[26]

In their speeches to the 1992 Conservative Party Conference, both John Patten and John Major emphasised the important of choice and diversity in state education. According to Mr Patten, the problems in education lay not with parents, not with teachers, but 'with the 1960s' theorists, with the trendy left and with the teachers' union bosses'.[27] The Prime Minister argued that: 'we want high standards, sound learning, diversity and choice in all our schools'. He went on to claim that in some – particularly those in the inner cities – 'Isaac Newton would not have learned to count; and William Wordsworth would never have learned to write'.[28] Mr Major did not, of course, explain how the creation of elitist schools in inner-city areas will do anything to improve the quality of education for *all* the children living there.

2. Furthering Diversity

In order to live up to its title, the *Choice and Diversity* White Paper, as we saw in Chapter One, proposes the creation of new types of school at the secondary level to operate *alongside* existing establishments. This is designed, in part, to provide a wider choice of school for parents (or, at least, *some* parents) in the maintained sector. But, at the same time, it marks a return to the modernising agenda of the early 1980s; for what the new schools have in common is an emphasis on technology as the all-important subject bridging the gap between academic and vocational courses.

As far as the CTCs are concerned, the government has had great difficulty finding generous sponsors and suitable sites, and the CTC to be opened in Bristol in the Autumn of 1993 will be the last of fifteen to adhere (at least in part) to the original blueprint. As we saw in Chapter One somewhat confusingly, the White Paper talks in terms of building on the work of the original CTCs by establishing *both* a network of maintained secondary schools with enhanced technology facilities, to be known as Technology Schools, and a network of schools established in partnership with business sponsors to be known as Technology Colleges. According to the White Paper, Technology Schools will become 'centres of excellence in technology teaching'; and the government has supported the initiative with capital allocations totalling £25 million in 1992-93 to fund additional equipment and building improvements to underpin the schools' curricular plans. Technology Colleges will offer a broad curriculum with an emphasis on science and technology, or on technology within other areas of the curriculum such as modern languages or business studies. It seems to be expected that most schools wishing to become Technology Colleges will do so as grant maintained schools. Business sponsors will be strongly represented on their governing bodies and will be able to play a direct role in their management. Unlike CTCs, these new Colleges will not be confined to urban areas.[29]

The first example of a new Technology *College* along the lines outlined in the White Paper is (again confusingly) the Lincoln *School* of Science and Technology, opened in 1992 and referred to briefly in

Chapter One. This is the product of a joint venture between forty local firms and Conservative-controlled Lincolnshire County Council. The new school (or 'education factory' as it was described in the *TES* in September 1992), is housed in an old high school which has been re-modelled and re-furbished at a cost of £3.5 million. Although, strictly speaking, the new school is maintained by the local authority, it is essentially run by the local firms. The industrialists appointed the first headteacher, have the majority of seats on the interim governing body, and have been given a major role in the planning of the curriculum which places special emphasis on information technology, enterprise and wealth creation. These same industrialists also plan to get involved in the day-to-day life of the school, acting as industrial tutors as well as arranging workshop activities for the pupils on real design and technology projects. Not surprisingly, the school has already attracted much hostility from local headteachers who claim it will damage neighbouring schools and point out that it undermines the government's stated aim of reducing surplus places.[30]

The new types of school do not feature as such in the Education Bill itself; but it is proposed that financial backing from individuals and companies can be used to establish new schools under the grant maintained system. Under the new legislation, parents, churches, faiths and voluntary bodies wishing to set up their own schools will be able to turn to private enterprise for help in finding 15 per cent of the building costs (as required under regulations covering 'voluntary aided' schools, now being used to legitimise this initiative). This is a significant new development, for, hitherto, opting for grant-maintained status has been confined to those schools wishing to leave local authority control.

With their clear emphasis on choice, diversity and

differentiation, the White Paper and the new Education Bill pick up themes which have preoccupied Conservative education ministers since 1979. Following the failure to re-introduce 11-plus selection in Solihull and elsewhere, Education Secretary Keith Joseph appeared on the ITV programme *Weekend World* in February 1984 to argue that: 'If it be so, as it is, that selection *between* schools is largely out, then I emphasise that there *must* be differentiation *within* schools.[31]

In fact, of course, Sir Keith was being too hasty in accepting defeat on the selection issue; for this government has found ways of creating differentiation *both* between *and* within schools. The new types of secondary school outlined in the White Paper, together with the CTCs and grant maintained schools already established, are clear attempts to foster the selection and differentiation that this government believes in; a more subtle and therefore potentially more sinister means to the same end is the promotion of the 'magnet school' concept among locally-maintained comprehensives.

The government has learned the lesson of the Solihull debacle of the early 1980s and will not now risk incurring the wrath of parents — particularly middle-class parents — by bringing back the 11-plus selection examination. So the new 'in-word' to replace *selection* appears to be *specialisation*. We are now to have the British version of the American 'magnet-school': in other words, *selection by specialisation*. And the details of this new 'schools revolution' were joyfully spelled out as the front-page story in the *Mail on Sunday* at the beginning of May 1992:

Education Secretary John Patten is looking at plans to turn secondary schools into centres of excellence in key subject areas ... This means

102

that some schools will specialise in the academic subjects like languages, maths and science; some will be technically-based; and others might offer performing arts or sport as their new specialism . . . The move puts selection back on the education agenda – but it drives a final nail in the coffin of the campaign to bring back grammar schools and the eleven-plus.[32]

And the Education Secretary himself argued in his article in the *New Statesman and Society*, published in July 1992, that socialists must now 'come to terms with the concept of specialisation':

. . . selection is not, and should not be, a great issue of the 1990s as it was in the 1960s. The S-word for Socialists to come to terms with is, rather 'Specialisation'. The fact is that children excel at different things; it is foolish to ignore it, and some schools may wish specifically to cater for these differences. Specialisation, underpinned by the National Curriculum, will be the answer for some – though not all – children, driven by aptitude and interest, as much as by ability . . .

It is clear that on to the foundation-stone of the National Curriculum can be built the liberation of all the talents through greater specialisation in our schools. This could be specialisation *within* a large comprehensive, setting for this or that subject – by the pupils self-selecting, or being guided towards their choice by aptitude and commitment. Or it could be something that builds on to the schools – a leading edge in bilingually-taught technology, for example, or in music, or where languages crucially meet business studies . . .

Such schools are already emerging. They will,

as much more than mere exotic educational bout-qiues, increasingly populate the educational land-scape of Britain at the end of the century, a century that introduced universal education at its outset; then tried to grade children like vegetables; then tried to treat them . . . like identical vegetables; and which never ever gave them the equality of intellectual nourishment that is now being offered by the National Curriculum, encouraged by test-ing, audited by regular inspection.[33]

The White Paper argues that specialisation should *not* be confused with straightforward selection: 'The fact that a school is strong in a particular field may well increase the demand to attend, but it does not necessarily follow that selective entry criteria have to be imposed by the school. The selection that takes place is parent-driven. The principle of open access remains.'[34]

This position is clearly disingenous; for in an area like Wandsworth in south London, which is already experimenting with the idea of its secondary schools being able to 'sell themselves' by having expertise in a particular curriculum area, it is obvious that two or three of the schools will find it easy to win the support of the 'right sort of parents' simply because their specialist strength gives them the status of revamped grammar schools. And the corollary of this is a growing number of disadvantaged schools, half-full of pupils who have no wish to be there. Indeed, Wandsworth administrators make clear reference to the hierarchy of schools that is developing nationally in their magnet schools publicity brochure:

Schools . . . could eventually fall into three groups. First, the elite high-performing schools: CTCs, opted out schools and local authority Magnet

Schools such as those planned by Wandsworth; then a larger group of 'run-of-the-mill' institutions delivering the standard National Curriculum; and, finally, the deprived 'sink' schools, mostly in the inner cities, with large numbers of pupils who speak English as a second language.[35]

And in a further twist to the story, the government announced at the end of October 1992 that schools could choose up to 10 per cent of pupils on the basis of musical, artistic or sporting ability. The DFE said that school governors need not follow the legal procedures needed to introduce academic selection because 'such choices would not significantly change the character of their schools'.[36]

All this makes it very clear that the comprehensive principle is under threat, and that what we face in the future is something which may prove even worse than the divided system of the postwar years.

Notes

1 Education Statistics for the United Kingdom, 1986, Table 17, p22, and *ibid.*, 1988, Table 18, p22; DES *Statistical Bulletin*, 6/88, May 1988.
2 *Daily Mail*, 13.5.87.
3 *TES*, 3.4.87.
4 Tony Edwards, Sharon Gerwirtz and Geoff Whitty, 'Whose Choice of Schools? Making Sense of City Technology Colleges' in Madeleine Arnot and Len Barton (eds), *Voicing Concerns: Sociological Perspectives on Contemporary Education Reform*, Wallingford, 1992, p144.
5 Stephen J Ball, *Politics and Policy Making in Education: Explorations in Policy Sociology*, London, 1990, p118.
6 DES, *City Technology Colleges: A New Choice of School*, October 1986, p5.
7 *Ibid.*
8 Geoffrey Walford and Henry Miller, *City Technology College*, Milton Keynes, 1991.
9 *TES*, 15.5.87.
10 *Guardian*, 23.5.87.
11 *Independent*, 14.9.87.

12 BBC *Panorama* programme 'A Class Revolution', 2 November 1987.

13 *Observer*, 20.9.87.

14 *TES*, 1.3.91.

15 BBC *On The Record*, 2.2.92.

16 *The Times*, 3.2.92.

17 *Ibid.*

18 *Observer*, 12.4.92.

19 DES, *Better Schools* (Cmnd 9469), March 1985, p3.

20 DES Statistical Bulletin 3/92, quoted by Paul Black, *op.cit.*

21 A McPherson and JD Willms, 'Comprehensive schooling is better and fairer', *Forum*, Vol 30, No 2, Spring 1988, pp 39-41.

22 H Glennerster and W Low, 'Education and the Welfare State: does it add up?' in J Hills *et al* (ed), *The State of Welfare: The Welfare State in Britain since 1974*, Oxford, pp28-87.

23 Tony Mooney, 'Sticking up for Comprehensives', *Education*, 13 November 1992.

24 'Education – All Our Futures', Speech by John Major to the Centre for Policy Studies at the Cafe Royal in London, 3 July 1991.

25 *Guardian*, 28.2.92.

26 John Patten, 'Who's afraid of the 'S' word?', *New Statesman and Society*, 17.7.92.

27 Speech by John Patten to the 109th Conservative Party Conference in Brighton, 7 October 1992, Chitty and Simon (eds), *Education Answers Back*, *op.cit.*

28 Speech by John Major to the 109th Conservative Party Conference in Brighton, 9 October 1992. A brief excerpt is in Chitty and Simon, *op.cit.*

29 DFE White Paper *Choice and Diversity: A New Framework for Schools*, Cm 2021, July 1992, pp45-46.

30 *TES*, 18.9.92.

31 Interview with Brian Walden, *Weekend World*, 12.2.84.

32 *Mail on Sunday*, 3.5.92.

33 John Patten, 'Who's afraid of the 'S' word?', *New Statesman and Society*, *op cit*, p10.

34 *Choice and Diversity*, p10 *op cit*.

35 Quoted by Anthony Green in 'Magnet Schools: Not So Attractive After All?' in *Forum*, Vol 33, No 2, Spring 1991, p40. This passage in the brochure is taken from an article by Stuart Maclure published in *The Sunday Times*, 18 June 1989.

36 *Guardian*, 30.10.92.

6
The National Curriculum Eroded

1. Curriculum Change Since 1988

Writing in the *Guardian* in July 1992 and reflecting on five years of Conservative policy-making, former Labour education spokesperson Jack Straw argued that:

> There could have been educational consensus around both the National Curriculum and LMS if the Tories had then consulted properly on their implementation. But in came CTCs and opt out schools, with the ostensible aim of opening up 'choice and opportunity', but with the practical effect of inflaming public opinion about a two-tier service: one side well-funded, the other starved of cash.[1]

It might well be true that the National Curriculum and Local Management of Schools represent two of the less divisive features of the 1988 Education Act, but, at least as far as the curriculum is concerned, the 'reform' process has been far from unproblematic. And in order to understand both the way in which news of the curriculum framework was received by teachers and local education authorities back in 1987-88 and the professional response to the numerous amendments introduced since that traumatic time, it is important to remind ourselves of the pre-ERA division of responsibilities.

Before 1988, practical issues concerning curriculum planning were the business of those curriculum specialists in local authorities and schools who had specific responsibility for shaping the learning programme. From the mid-1970s, a number of teachers and advisers were beginning to ask serious questions about the *purpose* and *scope* of the curriculum. Yet in only a minority of LEAs and schools was the term 'whole curriculum' sufficiently understood; and for too many pupils the curriculum on offer was something essentially *fragmented* or *partial*: a loose collection of subjects lacking either structure or coherence. Progress towards *whole-school* curriculum planning was certainly not uniform throughout the country; and pioneering schools and local authorities were not sufficiently evangelistic in getting the message across to teachers and parents. Nor was central government (loosely defined) actually speaking with one voice. The notion of curriculum coherence was endorsed by Her Majesty's Inspectorate in a number of curriculum reports published between 1977 and 1985, but it was not included in the DES 1985 White Paper *Better Schools* which laid down that the school curriculum should be: broad, balanced, relevant and differentiated.[2]

Emphasis on the concept of the whole curriculum represents a concern with the totality of experiences offered to all pupils. Coherence can then be seen as an active and continuous process of constructing meaning from the range of experiences offered. By 1988, only a minority of LEAs and schools had reviewed their programmes in response to this new philosophy of curricular coherence, though – at the design level – statements of entitlement had begun to appear from the early 1980s. As a recent report of a National Foundation of Educational Research (NFER) study of whole curriculum management points out, it was the 1988 Education Act which served to bring all these issues into the open 'partly by making public and explicit much that was previously left to local custom and practice, and partly by challenging the prevailing power structures of the educational system'.[3]

For the first time in the history of state education in this country, the 1988 Act established a single curriculum framework for all pupils aged five to sixteen. Yet this framework was conceived in great haste and this helps to explain why the original National Curriculum consultation document, published in July 1987, was greeted with a chorus of disapproval on the part of a large body of teachers and educationists.

Aware of the precarious nature of its support base, the Thatcher government was understandably reluctant to give publicity to the views of its critics and it was therefore left to Julian Haviland, former political editor of *The Times*, to publish (at the beginning of 1988) a book with the title *Take Care, Mr. Baker!* analysing the 20,000 or so replies which the DES had received in the wake of the spate of discussion documents which were issued while the 1987 Education Reform Bill was in preparation. Of these, over half (11,790) concentrated on the National Curriculum, and the government found it necessary to give a highly misleading impression of their overall flavour. The then Minister of State Angela Rumbold told a supporter on 19 January 1988 that of all the representations examined in the DES, only 1,536 were opposed to the idea of a national curriculum. As

Haviland points out, her answer was *accurate*, but it was also *incomplete*. The *principle* of a national curriculum *was* overwhelmingly approved in the replies; but there was not one response that endorsed *without reservation* the actual structure for the curriculum which the government was preparing.[4]

The 1987 consultation document was criticised by a number of teachers and lecturers for both its narrow, subject-based instrumental approach and its cynical disregard for the complexities of school curriculum planning. In an article in the *TES* published in September 1987, Professor Denis Lawton argues that:

> There is nothing wrong with subjects, provided they are treated as *means* and not as *ends*. Virtually all the enlightened views on curriculum planning are now agreed that subjects should be regarded as important *only* if they help to reach other objectives which, in turn, have to be justified ... All this is ignored in the government's consultation document: no justification is put forward for the selection of the foundation subjects; no arguments put forward to give priority to the core subjects; no attempt made to relate subjects to wider objectives.[5]

Similarly, the notion of a curriculum consisting of ten foundation subjects was characterised as both 'vague and mechanistic' in a letter from a group of academics at the University of Sussex published in the *Independent* in October 1987:

> The subjects listed seem to be no more than lumps extracted from the curriculum *status quo* which the government happens to approve of. What we need ... is some appreciation of the broad unifying categories (humanities, arts, sciences),

which, when placed properly together, might come to represent some kind of balance.[6]

As far as the primary sector was concerned, the government's simplistic framework was viewed by many as a clear rejection of that progressive primary-school approach to curriculum planning which refuses to endorse the secondary sector's obsession with artificial subject boundaries. In a speech delivered at the *Forum* Conference 'Unite for Education' held in London in March 1988, Michael Armstrong argued that primary teachers' philosophical objection to a subject-based curriculum was not simply a matter of the need to find room for the ubiquitous primary school 'topic':

It is rather that most of the really fruitful classroom inquiries, whether on the part of an individual child, a small group of children, or an entire class, have a way of moving in and out of subjects, conflating traditions, confusing boundaries, eliminating distinctions and creating new ones. So a study of the life of a frog becomes an exercise in philosophical speculation, scientific observation, literary fantasy and artistic method. So designing a set of earrings turns into an investigation of the psychology of faces. So an examination of mathematical powers embraces the geography of the universe and the mythical origins of the game of chess ... In learning ... all the significant insights tend to come to those, teachers and pupils alike, who refuse to be bounded by subjects, who are prepared to move freely *between* traditions and *beyond* traditions – from science to philosophy to art to some new field of inquiry – without embarrassment.[7]

So much, then, for the new National Curriculum's simplistic framework and general secondary bias. What was even more depressing was the almost total lack of rationale or curriculum philosophy in the 1987 consultation document, after more than ten years of constructive debate as to the most appropriate curriculum model for an age of comprehensive primary and secondary schools. In the words of Peter Watkins, the former Deputy Chief Executive of the National Curriculum Council, in a lecture delivered at the University of Birmingham in November 1991:

There is . . . one fundamental problem from which all others stem. The National Curriculum had no architect, only builders. Many people were surprised at the lack of sophistication in the original model: ten subjects, attainment targets and programmes of study defined in a few words in the 1987 Bill: that was all.[8]

In particular, the DES seemed determined to build on the principles outlined in *Better Schools* and ignore HMI advice on the essential nature of whole-school curriculum planning. As David Hargreaves pointed out in an article in the *TES* which appeared in January 1990:

One of the best ideas that Her Majesty's Inspectorate contributed to the [curriculum] debate was the principle that the curriculum should be 'broad, balanced and coherent'. The DES adopted the notion of breadth and balance, but somehow, and for unknown reasons, the concept of coherence was quietly dropped. Yet . . . it is one of the most important curriculum principles.[9]

Both the 1987 consultation document and the 1989 DES publication *National Curriculum: From Policy to Practice* saw the whole curriculum as a straightforward collection of subjects and failed to ask important questions about either the purpose of subjects or the totality of curriculum experiences to be offered to all pupils regardless of assumed ability. And the practice of establishing subject working groups, which were then left in virtual isolation to define their own parameters of subject content and status, served further to undermine the concept of curriculum coherence. Science, for example, as one of the first of the subjects to be developed, appropriated major sections of the traditional geography curriculum concerned with climatology and soil analysis. And this was by no means the only example of 'curriculum imperialism'. As Jim Sweetman has pointed out, several of the subject working groups adopted strategies – implemented at various levels of aware-ness – which served to sustain the specific subjects in ways which were 'diametrically opposed to any real cross-curricular perspective'. As a result, a curriculum framework was being constructed without either focus or direction – with dire consequences.

The School Examinations and Assessment Coun-cil (SEAC) and the National Curriculum Council (NCC) had responsibility for different aspects of the development process, but neither body had an overall view of the direction in which the curriculum was travelling or the facility to make metastructural links across a range of subjects . . . The result was predictable. An unteachable curriculum was developed where any desirable activity became compulsory.[10]

It was left to the National Curriculum Council, under

Duncan Graham's leadership, to make valiant efforts to lift the curriculum debate on to a higher plane. NCC Circular 6, published in October 1989, argued that:

> The whole curriculum of a school ... goes far beyond the formal timetable. It involves a range of policies and practices to promote the personal and social development of pupils, to accommodate different teaching and learning styles, to develop positive attitudes and values, and to forge an effective partnership with parents and the local community.[11]

The hierarchy of subjects in the National Curriculum would be left intact, but the subject-based framework would be given a horizontal overlay of *cross-curricular elements*. These were then outlined in the seminal NCC document, *Curriculum Guidance 3: The Whole Curriculum*, published in March 1990, which argued that the National Curriculum alone could *not* provide the broad and balanced curriculum to which *all* pupils were entitled. The elements needed to give the curriculum structure and coherence consisted of: cross-curricular *dimensions* (such as a commitment to providing equal opportunities for all pupils and a recognition that preparation for life in a multicultural society was relevant to all pupils); cross-curricular *skills* (oracy, literacy and numeracy, as well as problem-solving and study skills); and cross-curricular *themes* (economic and industrial understanding, careers education and guidance, health education, education for citizenship and environmental education). The document stressed that the successful management of the whole curriculum depended upon a corporate plan for the whole school, embracing all the aspects of the whole curriculum considered important by NCC and augmented by each school in the light of its individual circumstances.[12]

Yet while the NCC was working hard to provide guidance on whole curriculum planning, other developments were combining to undermine the concepts of structure and coherence, and this was particularly true in the case of the ever-changing pattern for Key Stage Four. Indeed, the last two years of compulsory schooling have rapidly become the most problematic area of the government's hastily-conceived curriculum plans.[13] It was clear, right from the start, that the National Curriculum's subject-centred approach would pose particular problems at Key Stage Four. Many teachers complained that it was simply not possible to fit all ten foundation subjects (and religious education), together with a number of cross-curricular themes, into a finite amount of curriculum time. Some talked of the risk of incurring pupil resentment and indiscipline. And as general economic prospects worsened, the argument re-surfaced that many of our problems would be solved if the secondary school curriculum could be re-structured in order to prepare pupils for the 'world of work'.

Speaking at the conference of the Society of Education Officers in London in January 1990, the then Education Secretary John MacGregor announced that he was reviewing the requirement that all schools should teach 14 to 16-year-olds all national curriculum subjects 'for a reasonable time'. In looking at 'a wider range of options' for these older students, he said he had asked vocational examination bodies such as the Business and Technician Education Council and the Royal Society of Arts to submit new qualifications for approval.[14]. Not surprisingly, the move was immediately rounded on by many headteachers who saw it as a step back to the days of 'GCE for the best and CSE for the rest'.

Then in an interview with the education correspondent of the *Daily Telegraph* at the end of October 1990, Education Minister Tim Eggar announced that the government had decided to encourage secondary schools to develop a vocational alternative to the academic curriculum. In his view:

> Far too many children from 14 upwards are studying things which they and their teachers do not regard as appropriate ... We have to offer these youngsters the sort of vocational courses and qualifications that will make sense to them – and encourage them to stay on in full-time education after the age of 16.

Schools would now be encouraged to develop parallel 'academic' and 'vocational' streams, with the main objective being to enhance the general status of vocational qualifications:

> That is the main issue facing us in education. That is the area where we are so much weaker than Germany – not in turning out graduates, but in producing skilled workers and supervisors ... To achieve that, we must now have two parallel streams – the vocational and the academic – from half-way through secondary school, so that children can concentrate on what interests them.[15]

The government might not at present be able to legislate for a return to the three-tier structure of grammar, technical and secondary modern schools embodied in the postwar settlement, but it should, in Mr Eggar's view, ensure that all the 'advantages' of that structure be made available to parents and pupils in the last decade of the century. That would mean

116

creating maximum differentiation within secondary schools.

Finally, Education Secretary Kenneth Clarke effectively abandoned Key Stage Four of the National Curriculum in his speech to the North of England Education Conference meeting in Leeds in January 1991. Ignoring NCC advice for *all* ten subjects of the National Curriculum to remain compulsory for all students to the age of 16, he announced that he had decided that only English, maths and science should remain 'sacrosanct' in the last two years of schooling. All students would still have to study technology and a modern language in addition to the 'core', but not necessarily to GCSE level. Of the remaining foundation subjects, students would study *either* history *or* geography, but art, music and physical education would become optional. According to Mr Clarke, the ten-subject curriculum up to fourteen was 'in itself a great enough leap for the English education system'.[16]

As Peter Watkins pointed out in his 1991 Birmingham lecture, the government's original proposals for Key Stage Four certainly ensured that the curriculum for fourteen to sixteen-year-old students would be more demanding and more rigorous and require the study of more subjects than hitherto; but 'that was in line with the practice of other countries, and it would keep open a variety of routes into education post-sixteen'. Now 'the National Curriculum is to all intents and purposes, dead beyond the end of Key Stage Three'. Mr Watkins acknowledges that the government is concerned to see a vocational element included for at least some pupils, though still harnessed to the National Curriculum; but he points out that it is not at all clear what this means:

There is doubt about whether the sort of qualifications hitherto provided by the vocational examining bodies are appropriate for schools and

117

whether they have the resources to offer them widely in any case. There is a danger that this could mark a return to an academic route for the able and a vocational route for the less able.

Granada Television's 1991 commission on education proposed channelling students at fourteen into one of three paths: academic, technical and vocational. Mr Watkins argues that this proposal too needs careful scrutiny for in the past 'all multi-track systems in England at whatever age have produced a hierarchy'. Can there ever be parity of esteem between the three routes?

While Key Stage Four was undergoing frantic adjustment, Kenneth Clarke was also planning to impose his views on teaching methods and classroom organisation on the nation's primary school teachers. Pandering to perceived public disquiet at the alleged prevalence of soft-centred progressivism, Mr Clarke made it clear throughout 1991 that he wanted to see a return to so-called traditional methods where primary pupils were 'streamed' from an early age and then taken through a programme of study in specific subjects. In an interview with David Tytler of *The Times* at the beginning of November 1991, he asserted: 'What has been regarded as good practice in primary schools in recent years can't deliver because it is too play-centred ... There is a great deal of this play-centred teaching ... which means at its weakest, there is a lot of the sticking together of egg boxes and playing in sand.'[17]

At the beginning of December 1991, the Education Secretary set up an enquiry into primary-school teaching methods and indicated that the report would be produced by the end of January 1992. The so-called Three Wise Men in charge of the investigation were asked: 'to review available evidence about the delivery of education in primary schools and to make recommendations about curriculum organisation, teaching methods and classroom practice appropriate for the successful delivery of the National Curriculum, particularly at Key Stage Two.'

The Report was prepared with great speed, and when it was published, it was hailed by the Education Secretary as a vindication of his earlier attacks on primary school methods. In actual fact, it refused to endorse one single method of grouping children and rejected the idea of class streaming. It also declined to outlaw topic work in schools and recommended that there would be 'a mix of good subject teaching and topic teaching'. One of the report's authors, Professor Robin Alexander of Leeds University, later complained that the Education Secretary had 'hijacked' and 'misinterpreted' the report for his own political purposes.[18]

2 The 1992 White Paper

There is very little specifically about the school curriculum in the 1992 Education Bill, but it features at various points in the White Paper *Choice and Diversity*, and the relevant paragraphs tell us a good deal about the general drift of the government's thinking.

In the first chapter, under the section entitled 'Imperatives for the 1990s', a concern is shown for 'children with exceptional ability' who 'should be advanced within the higher groups for all or part of the curriculum'. It is not clear exactly what this means in organisational terms; and there is also ambiguity about the following statement that 'the government has acted under the Education Reform Act 1988 so that, in addition to individual pupils, whole classes can also be allowed to progress as quickly as is educationally desirable'.[19] If this is meant to apply to primary schools, it contains all sorts of assumptions about the grouping of pupils, with the further implication that the National Curriculum is some sort of straitjacket which holds 'bright pupils back'.

The government is also concerned that some secondary schools should be encouraged to specialise in one or a small number of subjects, in addition to providing the full National Curriculum. The development of specialisation in a particular area will depend on the quality of teaching the school is able to offer and on the range of opportunities available for pupils to focus on that area. As we have already seen in Chapter Five, emphasis on the concept of specialisation is really a subtle means of re-introducing secondary selection and we can therefore treat with a fair degree of contempt the statement that the government will work to ensure that 'there are no tiers of schools within the maintained system, but rather parity of esteem between different schools, in order to offer parents a wealth of choice'.[20]

The White Paper lays particular stress on the place of the moral and spiritual dimension in school education, a subject known to be one of Mr Patten's pet concerns. Indeed, shortly after acquiring his new portfolio, the Education Secretary argued in an article in the *Spectator* (18 April 1992), that although 'we are all born with a sense of good and evil', schools can play an important part in helping us to choose 'whether to be good or bad'. The White Paper argues that 'proper regard should continue to be paid to the nation's Christian heritage and traditions in the context of both the religious education and collective worship provided in schools.'[21] And the arrival of the White Paper was swiftly followed by the publication (on 4 August 1992) of a consultation document aiming to ensure that religious education in schools 'reflects the fact that the religious traditions in Great Britain are in the main Christian'. Launching the document, Education Minister Baroness Blatch denounced the 'fruit cocktail' approach to religious education, where children are taught to understand the key principles of all the major faiths. According to one of the government's supporters, Colin Hart of the Christian Institute:

> There is evidence that in many school, religious education is not being taught at all. And where it is, Christianity is being watered down. Many of the new syllabuses are full of trendy jargon and multi-faith mish-mash. It is a disgrace. It has to be stamped out.[22]

The 1992 Bill gives grant maintained schools proper representation on the Standing Advisory Councils on Religious Education; and any grant maintained school which is currently required to teach the agreed syllabus adopted by the LEA in whose area it lies, will in future have the option of choosing to use any agreed syllabus.

3 Special Needs

As far as special needs provision is concerned, the new Bill proposes that local education authorities should retain responsibility for children with statements of special educational need, even if the majority of schools in their area have opted for grant maintained status. The Bill also lays out a new appeals system for dissatisfied parents and provides for the government to issue a code of practice to the LEAs. There is no reference in the original version of the Bill to the grant maintained special schools promised in Chapter Nine of the White Paper, but these may be added at a later stage.

The major criticism of this section of the Bill is likely to focus on the confusion as to who is actually responsible for special needs *as a whole*: grant-maintained schools or local education authorities. The 1978 Warnock Report estimated that around 20 per cent of children might at some time in their schooling have 'special educational needs'. In accordance with the provisions of the 1981 Education Act, the LEA has been required to maintain a 'statement' in the case of those children whose 'needs' are such as to necessitate special educational provision. The picture varies from one part of the country to another; but approximately 2 per cent of children are in special schools or similar provision – which roughly corresponds to the percentage of pupils with statements. So it is evident that the majority of pupils with special educational needs are in ordinary schools. While the new Bill makes it clear that local authorities are unquestionably in charge of the statementing process, this deals with only a small part of the problem. Whereas the 1981 Act attempted to legislate for a 'continuum of need', taking in all the most vulnerable children, it can be argued that the new legislation deals almost exclusively with those requiring special provision.

Speaking on behalf of the Special Educational Consortium – a group of around sixty special needs groups set up specifically to co-ordinate responses to the 1992 Bill – Philippa Russell from the Council for Disabled Children has said that the government has missed 'a golden opportunity to recognise that children's performance in school is actually affected by all sorts of factors in their external environment'. There is, she argues, no encouragement for health, social services and education departments to work together in the Bill despite the evidence that 'the most vulnerable pupils often need the help of all these agencies'.[23] The Consortium is campaigning for one body to be given clear and overall responsibility for the whole spectrum of special needs, not just statements. It also wants incentives for both LEA and grant maintained schools to cater for 'vulnerable children' so that schools do not feel tempted to abandon them in the interests of academic competition.

4 Where are we now?

Back in 1983, in the third of their influential Red Books, *Curriculum 11-16: Towards a Statement of Entitlement*, Her Majesty's Inspectorate argued that:

> The conviction has grown that all pupils are entitled to a broad compulsory common curriculum to the age of sixteen which introduces them to a range of experiences, makes them aware of the kind of society in which they are going to live and gives them the skills necessary to live in it. Any curriculum which fails to provide this balance and is overweighted in any particular direction, whether vocational, technical or academic, is to be seriously questioned. Any measures which restrict the access of all pupils to a wide-ranging curriculum or which focus too narrowly on specific skills are in direct conflict with the entitlement curriculum envisaged here.[24]

And the Hillcole Group publication *Changing the Future*, which appeared in 1991, argued that a national curriculum in a democratic society should be:

> Neither the 'secret garden' of the professionals, as in the past, nor the present centrally-imposed one. It should be based on a nationally-agreed

statement of entitlement arrived at through wide debate, but be flexible enough to be elaborated upon by educationalists, students, parents and community groups at a local level, to meet local needs. There would need to be a balance within the curriculum between the needs, aspirations and interests of the individual student and the needs of the community and wider world ... Access to knowledge, skills and understanding should not just occur through compartmentalised subject areas. Students should be offered the opportunity to see the links between areas of knowledge and to develop and transfer skills and concepts from one area to another.[25]

These are all curriculum principles to which most progressive teachers would subscribe. Yet with its failure to understand the concept of whole school curriculum planning, the clear approval of grouping by ability in the primary school, the virtual abandonment of the National Curriculum at Key Stage Four and the new and politically-motivated emphasis on specialisation and diversity at the secondary level, the government has effectively rejected all the principles which have underpinned good practice in schools since at least the late 1970s. It has allowed itself, as always, to be unduly influenced by the various pressure groups on the far right which reject the whole idea of an 'entitlement curriculum' and actually argue that grant-maintained schools should now be given the right to 'opt out of' the National Curriculum. The result is a flawed curriculum framework which needs constant adjustment simply in order to survive. Teachers will, of course, try hard to make the structure work, but it will always fall far short of a nationally agreed statement of a common curriculum.

Notes

1 *Guardian*, 7.7.92.
2 DES White Paper *Better Schools*, Cmnd 9469, March 1985, pp14-15.
3 Penelope Weston, Elizabeth Barrett and Jim Jamison, *The Quest for Coherence: Managing the Whole Curriculum 5-16*, Slough, 1992, p3.
4 Julian Haviland (ed), *Take Care, Mr Baker!*, London, 1988.
5 *TES*, 18 September 1987.
6 *Independent*, 14.10.87.
7 Reprinted in *Forum*, Vol 30, No 3, Summer 1988, pp74-76.
8 'The National Curriculum – An Agenda for the Nineties': Raymond Priestley Lecture delivered in the University of Birmingham School of Education, 14 November 1991. Reprinted in Chitty and Simon (eds), *Education Answers Back, op.cit.*.
9 *TES*, 26.1.90.
10 Jim Sweetman *The Complete Guide to the National Curriculum: Curriculum Confidential Two*, Newton Regis, 1991, p8.
11 NCC Circular Number Six, 'The National Curriculum and Whole Curriculum Planning: Preliminary Guidance', October 1989, p1.
12 NCC *Curriculum Guidance 3: The Whole Curriculum*, March 1990.
13 See Clyde Chitty 'Key Stage Four: the National Curriculum Abandoned?' in *Forum*, Vol 34, No 2, Spring 1992, pp38-40.
14 *TES*, 2.2.90.
15 *Daily Telegraph*, 30.10.90.
16 *Guardian*, 5.1.91.
17 *The Times*, 4.1.91.
18 *Independent on Sunday*, 2.2.92.
19 DFE White Paper *Choice and Diversity: A New Framework for Schools*, Cm 2021, July 1992, p12.
20 *Ibid*, p10.
21 *Ibid.*, p37.
22 *Daily Mail*, 4.8.92.
23 *TES*, 6.11.92.
24 DES *Curriculum 11-16: Towards a Statement of Entitlement: Curricular Reappraisal in Action* (HMI Red Book Three), 1983, p26.
25 Clyde Chitty (ed) *Changing the Future: Redprint for Education*, London, 1991, pp92-3.

7
Assessment and Testing: New Confrontations

1 Developments Since 1988

We saw earlier (Chapter Four) that the Education Bill makes provision for the dissolution of the National Curriculum Council (NC) and the School Examinations and Assessment Council (SEAC), and their replacement by a new powerful single body: the School Curriculum and Assessment Authority (SCAA) with up to fifteen members appointed, of course, by the Secretary of State.

Bringing together the management of curriculum and assessment could well be welcomed *in principle*. But if the school curriculum is thereby to become more examination and assessment led, the inevitable result will be to *lower* not *raise* general pupil achievement. And this looks likely to be the scenario for the immediate future, given the political complexion of the present government. For the story of assessment and testing since 1988 is one of a steady retreat from the only principles which make assessment a worthwhile activity.

Most of the right-wing pressure groups which played a part in the drafting of the 1988 Education Act were totally opposed to the idea of a national curriculum; they argued that a school's individual curriculum should be one of its selling points with parents. They were eventually persuaded to accept the new curriculum framework on the grounds that it would justify a massive programme of pupil testing at certain key stages, the results of which could then be used to reveal the strength of some schools and expose the shortcomings of others.

It seems clear that from the very beginning, Prime Minister Margaret Thatcher and Education Secretary Kenneth Baker disagreed strongly about the nature and purpose of external testing in the National Curriculum. The Prime Minister wanted externally set tests of a traditional kind; while Mr Baker accepted the need for an element of school-based assessment. It was eventually decided to set up the Task Group on Assessment and Testing (TGAT) under the leadership of Professor Paul Black, and this was given the very difficult task (in July 1987) of devising a workable scheme of assessment for the National Curriculum within six months. The first report was produced on 24 December 1987 and published in January 1988. Three supplementary reports followed at the end of March 1988; and a digest of the first report was also produced for discussion in schools.

The TGAT proposals were far more elaborate and sophisticated than anything envisaged by either Margaret Thatcher and her allies or the educational world in general. The particular approach which was adopted by Professor Black and his colleagues built on assessment procedures and practices already in existence, improving on them where appropriate and relating them to the specific new problems posed by the National Curriculum. One of the team's general assumptions was that, far from distracting classroom teachers from the teaching-learning process, good assessment would actually help teachers, and particularly primary school teachers, to know more about their pupils, and therefore to teach more effectively.

The two chief surprises in the TGAT proposals were the Standard Assessment Tasks (SATs) and the system of 'level of attainment'. The 'tasks' were designed as pieces of classroom activity and were meant to be sufficiently wide-ranging to avoid curricular distortion. The levels were designed to allow for differentiation, variation and progression. One very important aspect of the proposed structure lay in its rejection of the concept of simple, externally assembled 'pass/fail' tests, though Professor Black and his team accepted that the publication of school performance would have to be an integral part of the new system. The TGAT proposals can be viewed as an uneasy compromise between two conflicting purposes of assessment: appearing to find a role for professional expertise and showing a concern for *formative* assessment; while, at the same time, giving civil servants and politicians the sort of information necessary for the purposes of accountability, control and the efficient running of a market system of schools. Under the TGAT arrangements, pupil scores could still be aggregated to show results for a class, a school and even a whole LEA for comparative purposes. And from the government's point of view, this was the sort of information knowledgeable parents could then use to make their all-important judgements about the desirability or otherwise of individual schools.

After a few months of public debate, Kenneth Baker made an announcement in the House of Commons broadly accepting the TGAT recommendations. Then the 1989 DES publication *National Curriculum: From Policy to Practice* reported this commitment and set out a three-page description of the main features of the national assessment system. It appeared to most people that the government had accepted the major principles underpinning Professor Black's work. For according to the 1989 booklet:

> Assessment should be by a combination of national external tests and assessment by teachers ... The results of tests and other assessments should be used both *formatively* to help better teaching and to inform decisions about the next steps for a pupil, and *summatively* at ages 7, 11, 14 and 16 to inform parents about their child's progress ... Standard assessment tasks will be designed to be a support for learning, and will be drawn up under the direction of SEAC with the classroom context very much in mind. SATs for Key Stage One will each test attainment in a range of foundation subjects and will be designed to be administered unobtrusively. Teachers will be able to select from a bank of SATs those which most closely fit the sort of work they have been doing with their pupils.[1]

None of this fitted in with the philosophy of the right-wing think-tanks which began to develop their own alternatives to the authorised proposals. For example: in March 1988, the Centre for Policy Studies published a short pamphlet *Correct Core: Simple Curricula for English, Maths and Science*, which contained examples of what around 85 per cent of pupils could be expected to be able to do by the ages of seven, eleven, fourteen and sixteen.[2] And other groups conveyed to Brian Griffiths, Head of the Downing Street Policy Unit, their belief that short, time limited external tests were far more reliable than anything dreamed up by Professor Black and his colleagues.

The Prime Minister herself was persuaded by her

right-wing friends that the Education Secretary had allowed the government's assessment plans to be 'hijacked' by the detested educational 'establishment'. And we know from a letter from the Prime Minister's office to Kenneth Baker's private secretary, dated 21 January 1988 and leaked to the *Independent* in March, that Mrs Thatcher was profoundly unhappy with the main proposals in the TGAT Report. This letter outlined four of the Prime Minister's chief concerns. In the first place, it was argued that the Black Committee had designed an enormously elaborate and complex system which schools would find difficult to operate. Secondly, the Prime Minister was concerned that the tests would form only a part of the assessment process, and that the major purpose of assessment appeared to be *diagnostic* and *formative*, rather than *summative*. Thirdly, there was the problem of the overall costs of the exercise; and finally it was regretted that the new assessment system could not be introduced in less than five years.[3]

The story of assessment since 1988 has been that of the steady abandonment of the Task Group's sophisticated proposals, classroom teachers themselves and particularly those in the primary school – giving Mrs Thatcher a kind of 'posthumous' victory. For it can be argued that the right's preference for standardised, pencil-and-paper, 'objective' tests has been allowed to emerge triumphant largely because it has proved very difficult for overstretched teachers to implement the Task Group's complex structure.

There was piloting of tests for Key Stage One in 1990, based on the TGAT model, and then all seven-year-olds sat tests for the first time in 1991. By 1992, the tests had become considerably more straightforward; and there is a certain irony in the fact that at its conference in Bournemouth at the end of May 1992, the National Association of Head Teachers

(NAHT) passed a motion saying that the government's tests were now 'too simplistic to yield useful information about children's progress'.[4]

Former Education Secretary Kenneth Clarke was happy to view the outcome of the testing debate in 1992 as a 'defeat' for professional expertise. And he had already used his Westminster lecture delivered in June 1991 to launch an extraordinary attack on Professor Black's group suggesting that their 'complicated proposals' had been a foolish attempt to appease the government's misguided left-wing critics: 'The complications themselves were largely designed in the first place in an attempt to pacify opponents who feared above all else 'paper and pencil' tests ... This opposition to testing and examinations is largely based on a folk memory on the Left about the old debate on the eleven-plus and grammar schools.[5] No one could ever accuse Kenneth Clarke of showing any concern for the rules of reasoned argument and civilised debate.

The original TGAT proposals certainly contained many positive features and were designed to be models of good learning with assessment firmly built in. Nevertheless teachers found them very difficult to implement with scant resources and in a limited timescale. The more 'manageable' tests now being proposed will put enormous pressure on teachers to teach for such tests, a practice which will do irreparable damage to good learning practice. And, significantly, a letter from the National Association of Head Teachers and the Secondary Heads Association sent to the Education Secretary in the middle of November 1992 called for all tests for seven-year-olds to be scrapped. More recently, headteachers' associations and some governing bodies have supported teachers' calls to boycott the 1993 English tests for 14-year-olds.

2. GCSE and the Future of Course Work

Somewhat ironically, the text of the Chapter on 'Raising Standards' in the 1992 White Paper includes interesting references to improvements in sixteen-plus examination results over the past decade. For the GCSE examination, introduced in 1988, has been much criticised by the government over recent months for including too much coursework in its scheme of assessment and, by implication, for its reliance on assessment by teachers. And John Major himself intervened in the debate in his Speech to the Centre for Policy Studies delivered at the Café Royal in London in July 1991 (it is surely significant that the only audiences Conservative prime ministers and education secretaries seem happy to address are right-wing thinktanks). Mr Major argued that recent developments in the GCSE examination gave rise to a suspicion that standards were now at risk:

> It is clear that there is now far too much coursework, project work and teacher assessment in the GCSE. The remedy surely lies in getting GCSE back to being an externally assessed examination which is predominantly written. I am attracted to the idea that, for most subjects, a maximum of 20 per cent of the marks should be obtainable from coursework. This, of course, is the sound principle we have recently proposed for A-levels . . . And we must also ensure that GCSE is properly calibrated to challenge the most able. We short-change our brightest children if we devalue the currency of the exams they take . . . The same principles apply to that higher benchmark of excellence – the A-level. If the transition from GCSE to A-levels is now causing difficulties, we must level GCSE up, not lower

A-level standards.[6]

The GCSE was designed to provide a form of assessment suitable for use in all-ability comprehensive schools; and the coursework element was introduced to increase student motivation and thus achievement. The government's wish to see the examination simplified runs counter to these 'progressive' developments. The not infrequent calls for a return to GCE 'O' level (at least for the 'brightest' students) conveniently ignore the uncomfortable fact that this was the very examination, together with the CSE, which led to Britain having one of the lowest staying on rates in Europe. It is certainly difficult to 'manage' the assessment process in GCSE and to build up a national picture of standards; but these factors should not be used as reasons for moving back to more primitive forms of examining.

3 The Future of Inspection

The right of the Conservative Party has made no secret of its hostility towards Her Majesty's Inspectorate as an integral part of the so-called educational establishment; in Thatcher-speak, the Senior Chief Inspector has certainly not been 'one of us'. The Hillgate Group pamphlet *Whose Schools? A Radical Manifesto*, published in December 1986 argued the case for a full-scale investigation into the activities of the Inspectorate:

> We believe the time has come for a full and independent survey of the Inspectors, whose role has undergone considerable unsupervised change since the institution was first established in 1839. The only recent official survey is entirely bland, and seems to permit and to condone a far wider

range of activities on the part of HMI than has ever been expressly authorised by Parliament. We believe the time has come to define the procedures, criteria and accountability of the Inspectors, who are as likely as any other section of the educational establishment to be subverted by bureaucratic self-interest and fashionable ideology.[7]

In a later pamphlet, *The Reform of British Education*, published in September 1987, the ranks of those who were said to have worked hard to undermine traditional values in education and frustrate the pursuit of excellence were extended to embrace the civil servants of the DES. HMI advisers and DES civil servants must not, it was argued, be allowed to take control of the new statutory bodies set up as a result of the National Curriculum proposals in the 1987 Education Bill:

If so many bodies are really necessary, then we hope that several numbers of each of them will be appointed from *outside* the educational establishment, whose collective failure over the past decades has virtually *forced* the government to put forward its current reforms. And it is important that the proceedings of these bodies should not be dominated by the Secretariat provided by the DES, or by their HMI advisers . . . We regret that we have no confidence in the educational establishment, which has acted as an ideological interest group, and which is unlikely to further the government's aim of providing real education for all. It would be worth insisting that the new bodies should be enabled to function wholly independently of the DES, and with HMI present in an advisory capacity only.[8]

Kenneth Clarke was determined to undermine the power and authority of HMI, but, as we saw in Chapter Four, the Bill he had drafted to achieve this came unstuck in a spectacular fashion in the House of Lords on 2 March 1992. He was forced to backtrack on his plans and charge the Chief Inspector of Schools with the duty of selecting the inspection teams. Professor Stewart Sutherland, the new Chief Inspector and Head of OFSTED, will be the first to wield the new powers under the terms of the Education (Schools) Act, 1992, but it is still not clear how the new teams will be chosen. Vague promises of quality control have still to be translated into firm guarantees.

Inspections, as we have seen (Chapter Four) will take place every four years, starting with 1200 secondary inspections in 1993-94. In the following year, there will be a further 1200 secondary inspections, together with 4800 inspections of primary and special schools.

There is uncertainty as to whether Professor Sutherland can guarantee the quality of the inspection process with only a small number of HMI left to help him. As we have seen, there is also the vexed question of *publication* of the reports. OFSTED is required only to ensure that copies of the full report are sent to Professor Sutherland himself, the chairperson of governors and either the local authority of the DFE depending on whether or not the school has opted for grant maintained status. Summaries have to be sent to all the relevant parents and a full copy made available which could either be at the school or in the local library.

As with so many of this government's crude innovations, the new inspection framework has an air of improvisation about it. Yet schools, parents and pupils have surely had enough of being treated as guinea pigs. As David Tytler has pointed out in the

Guardian: 'The dangers of acting in this way can be seen in the confusion, frustration and resentment caused by the government's rethink on GCSE and the curriculum. Schools, pupils and parents have a right to expect that similar chaos will not dog the new inspectors.'[9]

Notes

1 DES *National Curriculum: From Policy to Practice*, 1989.
2 Sheila Lawlor, *Correct Core: Simple Curricula for English, Maths and Science*, CPS Policy Study No 93, March 1988.
3 *Independent*, 10.3.88.
4 *Guardian*, 28.5.92.
5 A fuller version of Kenneth Clarke's speech appears in Professor Paul Black's Presidential Address to the Education Section of the British Association for the Advancement of Science, given on 25 August 1992. Reprinted in Chitty and Simon (eds), *Education Answers Back, op.cit.*
6 'Education – All Our Futures', Speech delivered to the Centre for Policy Studies at the Café Royal in London, 3.7.91.
7 Hillgate Group, *Whose Schools? A Radical Manifesto* London, December 1986, p14.
8 Hillgate Group, *The Reform of British Education: From Principles to Practice*, London, September 1987, pp9-10.
9 *Guardian*, 13.9.92.

8

The Fightback and the Alternative

The Education Bill was published on 3 November 1992. In spite of the fact that very many of the roughly 850 responses to the White Paper, published in late July, were severely critical of several of the proposals made (particularly those concerning the Funding Agencies and their role *vis-a-vis* local authorities), the various clauses of the Bill itself simply re-presented these in legislative form. As in the case of the 1988 Act (ERA), no 'consultation' of any serious character had taken place – those wishing to contribute, and with a point of view, had wasted their efforts. This now began to seem normal procedure.

The Bill is of enormous length – even larger than ERA (and this had set a record for educational legislation). It contains 255 clauses as well as seventeen schedules, the whole covering 200 pages of closely packed print. It is expected to get even larger as it passes through parliament, primarily through the addition of government amendments expected as a result of hurried drafting.

The Bill is divided into six parts which in turn are divided into 'chapters'. It will be convenient to take these in turn.

Part 1: Chapter One, clauses one to six deal with the establishment of the two Funding Agencies (England and Wales). Chapter Two, clauses seven to fourteen detail the conditions where these Agencies assume part or full responsibility for the provision of school places.

Part 2: Chapter one, clause 14 defines a GM school; subsequent clauses (Chapter Two, clauses 16 to 29) prescribe procedures for county and voluntary schools to opt out, deal with such issues as the transfer of property and staff to the grant maintained governing body (Chapter Three, clauses 30 or 38), allow the establishment of new GM schools by 'promoters' or Funding Agencies (Chapter Four, clauses 40 to 46), and deal with the conduct of the grant maintained schools (Chapter Five, clauses 47 to 70). Chapter Six, clauses 71 to 84 are concerned with finance of grant maintained schools, and how these might change their character (Chapter Seven, clauses 85 to 92). Several clauses deal with the closure of GM schools (Chapter Eight, clauses 93 to 104). Chapter Nine, clauses 105 to 113, are concerned with provision for groups of opted out primary schools to have a single governing body. The rest of Part 2 is concerned with miscellaneous provisions relating to GM schools.

Part 3: This is entirely concerned with new provisions relating to children with special educational needs (clauses 139 to 168).

Part 4: This focuses entirely on provisions for school attendance, including duties of LEAs and parents (clauses 169 to 179).

Part 5: Chapter 1 is concerned with so-called 'failing' schools (clauses 180 to 188), and with arrangements following inspection. The next set of clauses (Chapter Two, clauses 189 to 204) deal with the setting up of education associations to run failing schools and other measures relating to these.

Part 6: This deals with LEA powers to propose significant changes of character to voluntary schools, and with powers of intervention by the Secretary of State as regards reduction of school places. It deals also with the abolition of the NCC and SEAC and the establishment of a new School Curriculum and Assessment Authority. It includes also the abolition of statutory education committees and limits the period when LEAs may supply services to GM schools to a maximum of two years (clauses 205 to 255).

The Bill also states that its implementation would not lead to any additional financial or manpower implications – basically because, it is claimed, increased costs at the centre would be offset by economies at local authority level, and by savings through the reduction of surplus school places.

It may be as well to bring together here the main measures in the Bill directed to enhancing the grant maintained sector, or, in plain language, increasing the number of opted out (or GMS) schools. Of course the main legislation providing for these was contained in the 1988 Education Act, while then, as now, the main lure provided was that of cash on the nail – or rather, simple and quite straightforward bribery by which parents, it was hoped, would put their own immediate interests, as they perceived them, before those of the community as a whole. However, in view presumably of the slow response, the Education Bill both attempts to ease the transition and to increase the number of GM schools without, in fact, involving parents (who have proved unsatisfactory) at all.

There are seven main measures in the Bill designed to increase the numbers of opted out schools. (1) It removes the 1988 Act's requirement that governing bodies must hold a second ballot before arranging a parental ballot on the issue. In other words the second ballot, held in 1988 to be desirable to avoid a rushed decision, is now held to be undesirable, and so is abolished. (2) The Bill very strictly limits LEA expenditure on publishing information for parents during or prior to a GM parental ballot. (3) The Bill provides for primary schools opting out in 'clusters' – such a cluster having a single governing body. The main two measures designed to increase the numbers of grant maintained schools, however, have each been briefly mentioned earlier: (4) 'Failing' schools, if and when rescued (and so not suffering closure) are to be automatically recruited to the GM sector; and (5) the proposed Funding Agencies may propose establishment of new GM schools, primary or secondary, according to whether one or both phases of education are within its remit in the area – it may also propose a new GM special school (Clause 40). (6), furthermore, under Clause 41 of the Bill, the initiative to set up a new GM school may be taken by people the Bill calls 'promoters', under similar conditions, but with the requirement also to consult the funding authority. What the Bill's promoters probably have in mind here (although this area is shrouded in mystery) is the establishment of the new Technology 'Colleges' referred to earlier, utilising the voluntary-aided category (see pp33-4).(7) There are, in addition (and finally) provisions to speed up the transfer of assets from an LEA to an approved GM school, and to strengthen the provisions preventing LEAs removing assets from schools approved for GM status. The latter measures have a punitive aroma.[1]

The Bill's Second Reading, and therefore the first full debate in the Commons, took place on 9 and 10 November, being finally carried with a majority of thirty-six. The debate was not remarkable, being characterised by a rigid adherence to and defence of the Bill's main measures by government spokespersons though opposition speakers probed weaknesses, stressing particularly the force of centralising measures. That this was a main feature of the Bill was indignantly denied by government speakers, in spite of its very clear tendency in this direction. The size of the government's vote showed that the Conservative Party, recently severely and publicly split on the Maastricht Treaty, saw the Bill as a means of unifying the party on a specific issue. Although there is certainly concern among some Conservatives, particularly those linked with shire county local government, this hardly expressed itself during the debate. And indeed Brian Cox has reported a widespread rumour that the Prime Minister, under severe pressure from the right on the European issue, had promised that, if right-wing MPs supported him on this matter they could have their way in education. If this is true, and it seems likely, it is an indication of the extent to which education has become a political football in quite a new sense. Now that the Secretary of State has so many over-riding powers including over the curriculum, the use of these powers as a counter in the unceasing political battles *within* (as well as between) political parties has become an important factor in the situation. This cannot be good for education.

The Bill then went for detailed discussion in a committee of the House of Commons. Due to the government's slim majority in the House as a whole, their majority on this committee, comprising about forty MPs, is only one. No serious amendments were made at the committee stage. Early in the new year the government brought in a guillotine motion severely restricting discussion, and the Bill received its Third Reading early in February. It then moved to the Lords where the committee is of the full House, so that over the early and mid-Summer of 1993 there will be several full discussions on the different parts of the Bill. It is here that united opposition, on some of the

141

key measures, may prove effective though, of course, amendments made here may be overturned later in the Commons.

As we write, criticism of the Bill is growing in the country as a whole as the full significance of this measure gradually sinks in. Parents' organisations, governors, teachers, trade unions and others are all deeply concerned at its implications, particularly as regards the government and control of education, as also of other matters. Apart from the clear intention of destroying local control of education and its planning, the Bill in fact contains few measures of any significance – perhaps the most important of these concern inspection and 'failing' schools. If the government has its way, most schools will become grant maintained – those remaining with the local authority will be inspected (as will GMSs as well, of course) and, if categorised as 'failing', will be 'dealt with' (an idea, incidentally, first announced by John Major to the Adam Smith Institute).[2] Some new types of school may emerge (the so-called technology schools and technology colleges). But otherwise all remains as before. There is no intention whatever, through this Bill, of increasing substantially the amount of resources devoted to education – indeed one of the Bill's virtues, according to the government, is that *no* extra resources will be required. Nothing is to be done to improve the admittedly scandalous state of pre-school education, where Britain lags far behind most European countries – in an area which research shows beyond any doubt to be crucial for children's overall development.[3] There is nothing on the controversial tertiary (sixteen to nineteen) stage where once again Britain lags very far behind Germany, France and other continental countries, even if the impact of heavy youth unemployment is now driving up the figures of young people staying on in full time education. Both these areas are of crucial significance for the future of this country. Both are totally ignored in this Bill.

What, then, is the alternative? Because of course there are alternatives – the country does not *have* to follow the myopic, and in some respects evil intentions outlined in this Bill. A policy for advance across the board in education, and a formulation of the principles behind such an advance has been set out by the Council for Educational Advance (CEA), a body uniting some 25 national organisations of parents, teachers, trade unions, the world of special education and others, of which one of the authors (BS) is currently president. This points to Britain's relative backwardness in education and proposes six 'building blocks' to modernise the system. These are:

(1) The provision of effective pre-school education for all.

(2) The provision of well resourced and fully staffed primary schools, teaching a revised, democratically controlled and effectively resourced national curriculum.

(3) The organisation of 11 to 16 secondary schools to meet the needs of the entire population, on the principle of comprehensive (that is, non-selective) education. Resource allocation for these should be based on the principle of equity having regard, however, to that of positive discrimination. A revised National Curriculum should be taught in all such schools – this must be seen, resourced and accepted as an 'Entitlement Curriculum'.

(4) The institution of a national plan for a tertiary education system (16 to 19) with a unified academic-vocational curriculum.

(5) A great expansion in higher education, under

democratic control, and adequately funded research.

(6) The guarantee of lifelong education, including paid educational leave.

In order to achieve such aims the CEA proposes that the following principles should underly development across the entire system:

(1) There should be a progressive rise in the funding of education to 6 per cent of GDP – nearer that of other EC countries.

(2) There should be equitable distribution of finance both between sectors of education (primary, secondary etc), and *within* each sector.

(3) All schools and school systems must be under some form of democratic, and so accountable, local control. State schools at present outside such control should be brought within it. This control must be exercised democratically – that is, through institutions of local government involving democratic electoral arrangements and representation. The relations between central and local government now urgently need a thorough review.

(4) There should be active steps to ensure the elimination of all forms of discrimination within the education system. This applies to differences of gender, social class, ethnic origin and age. There must be genuine equality of opportunity for all.

(5) Full scope must be offered to parents for creative involvement in the work of local schools and school systems. A properly constituted Home and School Association should be established in every school.

(6) Competition should be replaced by cooperation throughout the school system. Full co-operation between schools, local authorities, teachers,

parents, non-teaching staff and the community as a whole, is a healthier and more rewarding approach than the current stress on competition. Extension of the co-operative ethos in education is most likely to bring an effective renewal into our educational system.

Here, then, are the outlines of a policy which any government could begin to implement by a series of legislative measures, and which could ensure that, over a period, a modernised, flexible, high quality system of education for all was actually brought into being in this country – one of which we could be proud, and which would stand up well in comparison with similar systems across the Channel and the Atlantic. Each of the six stages outlined above are of equal importance – all need implementing. The six principles also outlined would ensure the construction of an equitable, fully democratic and resourced system. The CEA played an historic part in mobilising public support for Rab Butler's 1944 Act – indeed was brought into being at that time precisely to fulfil that function. Its programme for today, if implemented, would bring about a transformation equivalent to that of fifty years ago, but in modern terms – ensuring for Britain a well-educated, motivated and fulfilled population, ready to face the twenty-first century with confidence.

What are the prospects of moving in this direction? While the present government is in power, most people would answer – very little; and they would be right.

But there has been plenty of evidence recently of a strong surge of public opinion against reliance on market forces as the solution to all problems, economic and social. Surveys have shown very wide support for the principles embodied in the welfare state – Thatcherite individualist ideology has not succeeded in seriously denting these views. The official British

Social Attitudes Survey of November 1991 found 'an "astonishingly high" level of support for state provision of welfare services'. One striking finding was that those supporting a rise in spending on education increased from 50 per cent of those surveyed in 1983 to 60 per cent in 1990, 'it is now just behind health as the service the public wants most spent on'. More generally, raising taxes to fund services won the support of 32 per cent of those questioned in 1983, but of 54 per cent in 1990 (*Independent*, 21 November 1991). Further, various developments more recently – particularly the massive reaction to the threat of instant closure of the coal industry in response to market forces – have both eroded government confidence in itself and, more importantly, shown how the power of public opinion can force policy changes – or their promise. This itself is giving ordinary people more confidence to assert their views with increasing energy. The government has not (so far) attempted to close down *all* local authorities with one single blow, as it did in the case of the remaining pits in the coal industry. Instead, they have adopted a technique of slow strangulation. Our aim, in this book, is to show that this could be equally disastrous in its effects. Hence the importance of alerting people to the real significance of present measures.

As mentioned earlier, there are signs that resistance to current policy is hardening. Parents have been voting more consistently against opting out in recent ballots – the proportion of these resulting in defeat for this policy has increased; the recent significant majority against opting out among parents of the Prime Minister's old school, Rutlish in Merton, is a case in point. Further, the situation is more complex than appears at first sight. In the London borough of Wandsworth, for instance, three comprehensive schools have opted out specifically to remain comprehensive, and so avoid being sucked into Donald Naismith's (CEO) plan to turn all Wandsworth secondary schools into 'magnet' schools, thereby bringing back selection. The first school to take this road was the prestigious Milton Keynes comprehensive, threatened with possible re-organisation locally through bringing back a selective system, as proposed by Tory councillors. Some schools in Kent have taken a similar road. So even the opt out figures themselves comprise contradictory tendencies. Although some feel that such schools should not opt out (since this gives credence to the government's attack on local government), nevertheless the strength of feeling shown by local parents (and, usually, teachers, though these have no vote) in defence of comprehensive education is evident in these actions. They are witness to the extent to which parents generally continue to support, and defend, comprehensive education.

In spite of the pressure to divide, separate, and impose competition by each against all others, schools in some areas are creating their own organisation, or networks, to defend themselves against the malevolent effects of such unrestricted warfare in the battle for pupils (and so cash). In some areas as many as twenty-five schools are meeting together informally (as a 'consortium'), especially where they perceive their own authority to be at risk, to find ways of co-operating together precisely to obviate extreme forms of such competition. These are beginning to do their own quite informal planning as regards recruitment policy and catchment areas (see *TES* 17 April 1992). Such informal organisations, of course, have no statutory standing, but they are an interesting and potentially fruitful form of spontaneous growth in the present situation.

All such developments surely are to be welcomed. They represent a clear determination not to lie down under the unceasing blows directed against rational and co-operative endeavour. Such measures are paralleled by the current Parents' Initiative, which brings together, again informally, the main national parents' associations (with others) to concert plans to meet, and perhaps counter, current pressures from government. All such initiatives taking place both nationally and at the grassroots are to be encouraged. Governors organisations also clearly have a very important role to play in the new dispensation, and here also there are signs of a more active stirring in various parts of the country.

In his recent study, *The Role of Local Government in Education*, Stewart Ranson makes a close analysis of new developments here, based on four detailed case studies. He shows how, in the light of the extreme pressures now constricting these authorities, an active process of reconstitution has been going on. This is based on a new partnership between the authority on the one hand, and governors, teachers, parents and the public on the other, in which the former sets out primarily to serve the latter, identifying needs through consultation and together implementing agreed solutions. Many examples are given of the creative nature of this partnership in spite of the fact that, as Ranson points out, central government has deprived the LEA of many of its traditional powers (p165). Nevertheless the author concludes his study on a note of optimism. The four authorities (Enfield, Kent, Manchester and Warwickshire) 'exemplify the tradition of creative innovation' in the reform of local education which, in his view, has been highly impressive (p186). They illustrate, he adds, 'the conditions for the effective working of a reformed education service'. Each LEA 'has brought a distinctive perspective to the management of change' that derives from consideration 'of local needs and demands'. Only 'a very sophisticated social institution could bring off this demanding task'.

The four exemplar LEAs studied 'have gone a long way to realising these exacting demands in the public domain'. Close reading of the case studies does indeed reveal a truly impressive transformation and level of service.[4]

The present government is clearly determined to destroy all such development and bring local control of education to an end – and all in the name of radical 'reform'. This is an act of vandalism without any parallel in educational history. Very recently Duncan Graham has added his protest against what is happening. LEAs work in implementing, and supporting, the National Curriculum and assessment has been exemplary, he writes. 'It is difficult to see how they could have made a better start in their new role: and yet it is being taken from them before their performance can be judged'. This is 'a massive and wilful sacrifice of resources and people which is hard to justify on rational grounds'. In my judgement, he concludes, local authorities could and should be 'the basis of the future'. Local government is 'too important to be cast aside as it has been'. If the government now yet further reduces LEA powers, he concludes 'at stake is a loss of partnership that will leave "a huge gap" in the way schools are supported and monitored'. 'The quiet mediator, the reassuring adviser, that is what schools will miss most'.[5]

The government, we know by now very well indeed, will pay no attention whatever to this expertly grounded and knowledgeable advice, unless somehow forced to. That it is deadly serious on this issue is very clear indeed from the fact that Clause 245 (almost the very last, located under the heading 'miscellaneous') of its execrable Bill, removes the statutory duty on local authorities to appoint an education committee, as laid down in the 1944 Education Act. The abolition of an education committee to all intents and purposes implies the end of the local *education* authority, even if residuary duties relating to education are carried out by other committees. So, far from building on the 1944 Act, as government spokespersons proclaim, this Bill sets out deliberately to destroy some of its most crucial measures. The White Paper actually refers to education committees as 'statutory obstacles' to organisational flexibility (para 6.5).

So short-sighted an attitude, or objective, is almost unbelievable. It is hardly surprising, then, that some of the best people working in this field are going, not wishing in any sense to be linked with the acts of destruction now taking place. At the end of November 1992 it was reported that Robert Bevan, Director of Education for Powys, resigned his job 'in protest at government policies'. Introducing a market system in education, he said, 'means that there will be winners and losers', and 'the losers are likely to be those children in greatest need'. He also forecast that local democracy in the education service would vanish 'within the next few years' (*TES*, 20 November 1992).

This is, of course, an individual solution, and it is understandable. But in the present situation, we believe, LEAs must follow the example of those studied by Ranson and, far from giving up the fight, actively search out new ways of preserving their role and, if possible, enhancing it. There is no doubt that schools and school systems in the areas of very many authorities appreciate the cohesion, partnership and the opportunities that their relationship supplies. In very many LEAs there is no serious desire among schools to become independent, isolated units competing against all others. Rather the opposite. This is increasingly realised and understood. Basically, this is why there has been no rush to opt out following the election, even given the extent of the cash lure, or bribes now on offer. It is as simple as that.

We cited, at the start of this book, a letter from an embattled chief education officer expressing his own passionate feeling that what is happening 'is not only damaging to education but fundamentally challenges the whole notion of democracy in this country'. There are, he warns, 'far too few people aware of the nature of the changes that this government is bringing about'. The country as a whole, he concludes, 'and education in particular, will be the losers over the next 5-8 years'.

We agree.

That is why we have written this book.

Notes

1 *At First Reading: the Education Bill 1992*, a commentary by Dr Robert Morris and Elizabeth Reid, AMA and ACC, 1992.
2 This was reported in the *Guardian*. Major's announcement was made at the fifteenth anniversary dinner of the right-wing Adam Smith Institute; his audience had paid £100 per head for the dinner held at the Banqueting House, Whitehall (guests being both right-wing and well-heeled). The proposal for failing schools, first announced here, was explained by a Whitehall source as being derived from the private sector's handling of bankrupt companies: 'The principle of the new scheme is to declare the school academically bankrupt and bring in the liquidators and a new management capable of taking over the failed school', he said. There is something inexpressibly ironic about such an audience in such a place confabulating about what to do about failed inner city schools mainly, presumably, in the Midlands and North. The two groups concerned could hardly be more distant both in space and understanding. However, Major took the opportunity to reassure 'deprived' children at this 'banquet' as well. 'Education is the key to the opportunity society', he said. 'We mean to end for good – and I mean for good – the giant left-wing experiment in levelling down.' 'This', he went on, 'will not only help the gifted but perhaps more importantly, the less gifted and deprived as well'. *Guardian*, 17.6.92.
3 For the latest expert assessment, see Gillian Pugh, 'A Country That Couldn't Care Less?', *TES*, 13.11.92.
4 Stewart Ranson, *The Role of Local Government in Education*, London 1992, especially Chapter Seven, 'The LEA and the Future'.

5 Duncan Graham with David Tytler, *A Lesson For Us All: the Making of the National Curriculum*, as reported in *Education*, 6.11.92. Unfortunately this book was published too late for us to make proper use of it here.